EL ESCORIAL

THE MONASTERY
AND THE PRINCE'S AND INFANT'S
LITTLE HOUSES

EL ESCORIAL

THE MONASTERY
AND THE PRINCE'S AND INFANT'S
LITTLE HOUSES

TEXT AND NOTES

BY

MATILDE LOPEZ SERRANO

MADRID

EDITORIAL «PATRIMONIO NACIONAL»

1984

1. Door and Main Entrance.
2. Porch; the Library on the first floor.
3. Courtyard of the Kings.
4-5. Staircases which lead to the Basilica and its façade.
6. Porch or vestibule of the Basilica.
7. Atrium of the Temple or Low Choir.
8. Courtyard.
9. Choirs of the Seminaries.
10. Basilica.
11-12. Presbitery and High Altar.
13. Royal Oratories.
14. Staircase which leads to the Choir and entrance to Pantheons.
15. Antesacristy.
16. Sacristy.
17. Altar of the Sacred Form.
18. Capitulary Halls.
19. Main Lower Cloister.
20. Court of the Evangelists.
21. Old Church.
22. Main Staircase.
23. Hall of the Trinity.
24. Hall of Secrets, ancient porter's lodge.
25. Entrance and ascent to the Main Library through. Porch No. 2.
26. Library of manuscripts.
27. College.
28. Entrance to the Palace of the Bourbons.
29. Staircase of the Palace.
30. Rooms of the Palace.
31. Door which leads out of the Palace and ascent to that of the XVI Century.
32. Hall of Battles.
33. Apartments of the Infanta Isabel Clara Eugenia.
34. Gallery of the Royal Chambers.
35. The throne Room.
36. Apartments of Philip II.
37. Bedroom and Oratory of the King.
38. Courtyard of the Masks.

N

LONJA

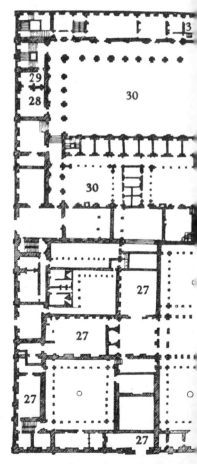

Part of the College

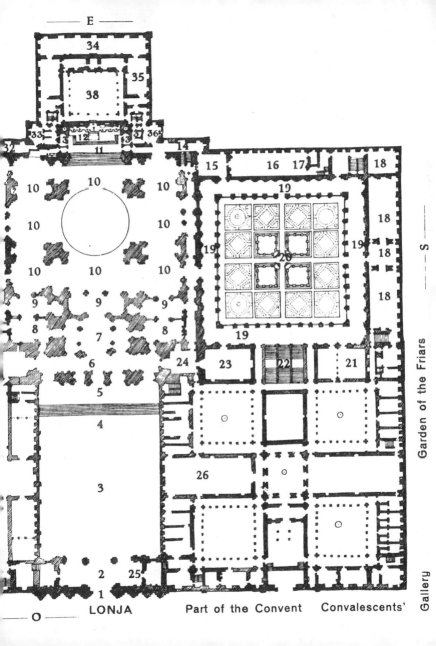

E

34

35

38

33 3 12 3 36

32

11

14

15 16 17 18

19

10   10   10

10   10   18

10   10   19   18

20   19   18

10   10

9   9   9   18

8   8

7

6   19

5

24   23   22   21

4

26

2 25

1

LONJA   Part of the Convent   Convalescents'

Garden of the Friars

S

Gallery

O

THE MONASTERY OF SAN LORENZO DE EL ESCORIAL

THE visit to the Monastery of San Lorenzo de El Escorial is a must for all kinds of tourists; the grand, austere majesty of its architecture, the vast artistic riches contained within and the high historical magnificence of its creation and subsequent development in national life, make it one of the most extraordinary monuments in Spain; in its time, it soon came to be known as the «eighth wonder of the world» **(p. 17).**

The year 1963 was a decisive one for the Monastery of San Lorenzo de El Escorial, for the high governing body which looks after it, with unequalled effort, and supported by the Ministries to which it was attached, gave a grant for the reconstruction, restoration, preservation and embellishment which the importance of the monument demanded. The same year saw the fourth centenary of its construction, and from then on the immense project was completed in an unbelievably brief and intense period of time.

In such an article as this, it is almost impossible in so short a space to convey any impression of the tremendous work which was accomplished, but nor can we overlook it. Just a simple enumeration of centenary achievements will suffice to convey to the reader not only the effort which was made to restore the Monastery to its original, primitive state, but also the effort which was made to improve and beautify the entire edifice.

In the words of the architect himself who was in charge of the restoration, Don Ramón Andrada, Head of the architectural Department of the National Trust, "so important have been the works that one can safely maintain that, after the great reconstruction ordered by Charles II to repair the damage which the Monastery suffered in the fire of 1671, the year 1963 marks another of those moments of climax in the life of the Monument, for it was in this very year that it reached the fourth centenary of its reconstruction and, moreover, the works which had been planned and the necessary, far-reaching repairs which had been undertaken in order to avoid ruin and destruction, and which ordinary means and usual methods of preservation and undertaking would have been unable to rectify, were completed. What is more, further works of reconstruction were able to be completed for a bigger exhibition and larger public, works which were made necessary and demanded by the affluence of its visitors (about half a million) who come annually to admire the riches which the Monastery contains: works which are enforced by the Museum technique".

So, apart from the incessant struggle against termites, the Jardín de los Frailes has been replanted in new ground, and they have drained and strengthened the whole of the corner towers as much as their magnificent chapters, "already restored under Charles II, according to the plan submitted by Bartolomé Zumbigo, who modified their outline, cementing them together and heightening them to almost 4 metres above their original size, to a height which has remained the same ever since". (Andrada). The so-called *Palacio de Verano (Summer Palace) of Philip II*, which stands on the lower floor and which corresponds exactly to the Sixteenth Century Palace on the upper floor, is being used once more, and has been converted into a Picture Gallery, just like the two halls in the gallery of

the Palace Patio or the Chancery; a new slope down to the
Pantheon of the Kings has been discovered; the Patio de los
Mascarones (Courtyard of the Masks), or private courtyard in
Philip II's Palace, the oldest in the building, judging from the
evidence of the first architect, Juan Bautista de Toledo, has
been restored; and the so-called *Vaulted Floor* has been con-
verted, with excellent atmosphere, into a *Museum* of the
Monastery's Architecture.

Yet another achievement is the Hall of Conference, or Lec-
ture Hall in the main high cloister on the right hand side of the
main staircase and with balconies which overlook the Jardín
de los Frailes. Although its furnishings are, of course, modern,
yet still fit in with the atmosphere, its walls have been decorated with the eight tapestries from the series known as *"los
Monos" (the Monkeys)*, for these are the most characteristic
of the animals which appear in them —amongst the flowers,
the fruits, the little garlanded branches, and others which look
like wooden arbours. The tapestry is Flemish, dating from the
Sixteenth Century, very delicate and woven with an abundance
of fold thread.

As for the "lesser" works, one must mention the restoration
of the Lonja pavement and that of the Patio de los Reyes
(Courtyard of the Kings). The best ones have been carried out
in the water-gratings and the drainage systems, increasing the
number of water closets. Special mention must be made of the
new, powerful electrical installations which give adequate
illumination to the exhibition halls (Picture Gallery, Museum of
the Monastery's Architecture, Sacristy, Chapter Halls in the
Basilica partly and fully, façade and portal, vaults, high altar
and groups of royal tombs, low altars, choir and organs beneath the dome) also to the main cloister, with the paintings
on the vaults, and the staircase of honour; to the Library

(paintings of the vaults and stained glass windows in the centre); to the Pantheons and the Sixteenth and Eighteenth Century Palaces. The courtyards have also been illuminated and this brings about some delightful and splendid effects which correspond at the same time both to the Courtyard of the Evangelists and to the Courtyard of the Kings.

Finally there is the extraordinary exterior illumination of the Monastery which strikes the eye not only with the harmonious massiveness of the building (facades) but also with all the movement of its magnificent fantastic architectonic distribution (dome, towers, columns, slate roofs). The same thing happens with the illumination of the gardens and orchards which

Lastly, and next to the mass of architectural and engineering restorations, one must mention the restoration of the basilica organs which have been able to give splendid concerts. A beautiful chiming bell has been attached to the tower clock.

*   *   *

San Lorenzo de El Escorial is 49 kilometres by road from Madrid. It is situated right next to the Guadarrama mountains at a height of 1.055 metres. The town of San Lorenzo de El Escorial (7.000 inhabitants) which rises up around it, is a pleasant, peaceful spot during the year and becomes a lively centre during the summer. Its picturesque surroundings heighten to a greater extent the powerful architecture of the monastery; the mountains of the Sierra de Guadarrama rise up to the North and West; to the East and South the plain of Castile stretches as far as Madrid.

The building of the Monastery was King Philip II's own idea, for he wanted in this way to commemmorate the victory of the battle of San Quintín which was won for Spain on the 10th of August, 1557, the feast-day of San Lorenzo. The King, a devout worshipper of the saint, as an act of thanksgiving, dedicated the monastery in his name. First and foremost the Monastery had to be a Royal Pantheon, a sepulchre for his ancestors, for himself and for his family. He established a Community to look after the Monastery and to attend to the spiritual and material needs of the foundation. The selected order was that of the Hieronymites, chosen because they were Spanish and because it was the very order which had accompanied the old Emperor Charles V in Yuste. At the same time, Philip II wanted a residence which he could use as a Palace of rest. His preference for it was so great that it was there that he chose to die (on the 13th of September, 1598).

The works of construction lasted for 21 years (from the 23rd of April, 1563, to the 13th of September 1584). The architect in charge of them was *Juan Bautista de Toledo,* who had as his assistant *Juan de Herrera* who, on the death of the former, took his place and accomplished a magnificent work with a very personal style, "with a strict purification of the classical elements of the Italian Renaissance", an inspired anticipation of modern architectonic concepts, which has been regarded as an extremely faithful interpretation of the King's original idea. The King also wanted to make the Monastery of El Escorial into a compendium, housing a selection of the Arts and Belles Lettres of his time. To this end he gathered together a large group of Italian and Spanish artists who accomplished the interior decoration: Tibaldi, Luchetto, Granello, Zúccaro, Cincinato, Sánchez Coello, Navarrete el Mudo (dumb), Monegro, etc. Other great artist worked for him without scarcely leaving their respective studios, as, for example, the Milanese sculptors in bronze, León and Pompeyo Leoni, Titian and El Greco.

The Monastery is a gigantic rectangular parallelogram (207 metres by 161 metres) with four towers of 55 metres at each corner, covered by slate columns on top of which are large metal globes (1,40 m. in diameter) with a weather vane and a cross **(p. 17)**. On the eastern side of the parallelogram, in the centre, protrudes the upper part of the temple and the rooms of Philip II's Palace, and because of this it is popularly pointed out that the Monastery resembles the shape of a gridiron, the instrument used in the martyrdom of San Lorenzo. Also, projecting above the building are the two 72 metres twin belfies and the magnificent dome, or cupola of the temple which, in its largest dimension, reaches a height of 92 metres. In the building, the greater part of which is of Doric style and fashioned in granite, 9 towers rise up, and there are 15 cloisters, 16 patios, 88 fountains, 86 staircases, more than 1200 doors and 2600 windows.

A wide esplanade, called *La Lonja,* encloses it on its northern and western sides at a width of 36 and 52 metres respectively, an esplanade which ends in an enclosure of carved granite ornamented with sturdy pilasters surmounted with globes. Its nine entrances are secured with thick iron chains. The ground is divided up by paths made of perpendicular granite flagstones which correspond to the pilasters and doors of the building (see Cover) **(Page 18).**

To cater for the need of Court lodging quarters and services, the so-called Official Houses, Ministries houses for the Infantes, the Queen and family were built around the Lonja, at the edge of the Pavement, linked one to the other by communicating arches (except the House of the Infantes), all made of granite and of a simple architecture which harmonizes with that of the Monastery. An underground passage called La Mina (mine) crosses La Lonja on its Northern side from the Official Houses to the portal of the Palace of the Bourbons, a passage which was constructed in the time of Charles III to avoid the discomfort of sharp winds ans snowstorms during the winter. The House of the Infantes and that of the Family are linked to the Monastery by a passage which protects La Lonja from the west wind on its southern side, a passage constructed similarly from granite, covered over with slate and decorated with pilasters, windows and arches.

On the eastern and southern sides an enormous terrace, 28 metres wide and 547 metres long, supported by 77 arches made from quarried stone, nearly 8 metres high, and ending with a parapet or balcony made of carved stonework, corresponds to *La Lonja.* Between this terrace and the building stretch beautiful gardens in which pruned box trees or shaped rose bays form geometrical patterns very pleasant to look at, and into the patterns which they make are inserted twelve simple fountains with large, square water basins, in the centre of which the water springs from a spout, also made of granite. These have been called *hanging* gardens because they are built upon arches supported by pilasters which form little shrines, recesses and pleasant seats for those who come down the steps —which also serve to communicate with the surrounding orchards and woods.

Facades

In the centre of the immense pattern formed by Las Lonjas and the terraces rises the magnificent massiveness of the monastery, whose facades present an unequal architectonic and artistic interest. The *eastern façade* **(p. 33)** is the simplest of all and in its centre rises the structure of the almost square building which constitutes the Sixteenth Century Palace. On its back or west wall there rises a smooth frontispiece without windows or adornments, which forms the back of the Main Chapel. At both ends of the facade there are two square towers. The wall fronts are decorated with five series of windows, except those of the Palace which have only two, adding up to a total of 286 windows and a further five doors, two in the towers, another two at the sides of the Sixteenth Century Palace, and the other, which is also a grating, in the middle of it.

The *northern façade* **(p. 18)** is 162 metres in lenght, and its wall face is divided into equal spaces by striking pilasters which project as far as the cornice. Between these there open four series of windows, 180 in all, and three large doors, the middle one, which is the old Palace door; the one on the right which leads to the Colegio de PP. Agustinos; and the one on the left leading to the Royal rooms. A fourth very small door, in the *Torre de las Damas,* was the one which Philip II always used because next to it is the old main staircase of the Palace.

The *Mediodía façade* (southern) **(p. 20-21-36-37)** is the most beautiful of all, not only because of its magnificent simplicity, bue because, as a result of the difference in the ground level, it is taller. Like the northern one, it has along its entire length of 162 metres an archway five metres in height which rises over the terrace of the gardens until it meets the level of La Lonja, an archway decorated with square, barred windows. Moreover, the facade has four series of windows, the first of these with protruding iron bars. In all there are 296 windows. There are also three small doors, one in each tower and the third one in the centre. Next to this facade stands the most beautiful of the above-mentioned gardens, the one known as the *Jardín de los Frailes* (**p. 20-21-36-37**) from whence one may enjoy a unique view of the whole of the southern side of the building, with the hills and the sierra on one side, and the vast plain stretching to Madrid on the other; at the foot lies the large lake or reservoir, a mirror in which the Monastery is perpetually reflected, together with the marvellous, ever-changing plays of light as the hours pass... The beauty of this façade is further enhanced by the *Galería de Convalecientes* (**p. 20-21-36-37**) which corners on to it and to the western façade, remaining completely independent from the Monastery building. It earned its name because, being on the same floor and adjoining the infirmary, protected from the North and West and open to the South and the East, it served as promenade for the convalescents who could enjoy the temperate and healthy air and the beautiful views which it offers.

The entire Galería, as has already been mentioned, is independent from the outline of the Monastery, for its back wall is pulled out from the Apothecary's corner (a corner formed by the South and the West) and attached to it by a large balcony with iron railings, fixed above the cornice of the cellars, and for this reason it is a little widened. The Galería is some 5 metres wide by 26 metres long in the eastern direction and somewhat more in the Mediodía direction. It forms two structures or galleries. The lower one, on a level with the gardens, is of Doric style with eight arches upon columns and with some arched intercolumniations. In the back wall are set recesses of two sizes, and the smaller are made into seats. The higher gallery is of Ionic style with a stone balustrade and parapets and finishes in an architrave, frieze and cornice with indents —a neat work of exquisite elegance. Its creator is Juan de Herrera who expresses it thus in his *"Explanation of the designs for the*

Monastery of El Escorial" (1589), sketches drawn with his own hand and engraved by the Flemish Pedro Perret with the authorization of Philip II, a text and illustrations so rare that they have not been readily attainable for the investigator, and this has given rise to erroneous attributions.

The *main façade* **(pages 18-19)** or western facade (207 metres long by 20 high) has its wall divided into equal spaces by protruding pilasters which break up the portals with two upright structures finishing in a cornice. The elegant portal, also in two structures, (Doric in its first span and Ionic in its second, with its frontispiece completed with globes) projects from the centre of the facade, with the main door. Above this is a small window, flanked by slate, the emblem of the martyrdom of San Lorenzo and of the Monastery of El Escorial. In the centre of the upper structure protrudes the royal shield of Philip II and in a recess is a statue of San Lorenzo (4 metres high) carved from granite, with the head and hands of white marble, the work of Juan Bautista Monegro, a sculptor from Toledo and an architect contemporary with the work of El Escorial. This entrance leads to the Monastery through a wide porch or portal which in turn leads to the *Patio de los Reyes* **(p. 23),** so called because of the 6 large 5 metre high statues of the monarch of Judah: from left to right, Jehosophat, Hezekiah, David, Solomon, Josiah and Manasseh which adorn the facade of the temple. These are also the work of Monegro who used the same materials, granite and marble, as he used for the statue of San Lorenzo; the crowns, sceptres and insignia are of gilded bronze and are the work of the sculptor Sebastián Fernández; the inscriptions by each statue were placed there in 1660.

The patio is perfectly proportioned, 64 metres long by 38 wide; four series of windows open on to it, 80 on each side.

As one looks towards the church, between the eighth and ninth windows in the left hand wall, one can find the last stone used in the building, indicated by a small black cross to which corresponds another large cross in the roof, formed by the cut of the slates. One should also notice the fine facade of the porch or portal which leads to the patio, as it has a cleverly arranged set of windows which corresponds to the two rooms of the main Library and the Manuscript Library.

The Basilica

At the end of the Patio, built upon a spacious platform which is approached by seven steps which occupy the entire width of it, stands the splendid *basilica*. The *facade* is Doric and consists of two structures with towers on either side. In the lower structure there are five arches set between large pillars and on top of these runs a gallery with an iron railing; above this runs the wide cornice which forms the basis for the upper structures; surmounted upon this are the pedestals with the six statues of the Kings of Israel and their respective inscriptions. The pedestals are joined together by a small iron railing, and set in the wall there are three rectangular windows, finishing with a frontispiece broken in the middle by another large window which sheds light upon the choir and the church. The towers, 72 metres high, are partly incorporated into the building, for which reason they seem to be lower; they end in pyramids, with metal globes upon cupolas; the bells and the clock are found in the rigth hand tower **(p. 17-34).**

Monasterio: Vista general panorámica
Le Monastère: Vue d'ensemble
Monastery: General panoramic view

Kloster: Allgemeiner Rundblick
Monastero: Vista generale panoramica
Mosteiro: Vista geral panorâmica

17

Fachàdas norte y poniente
Façades Nord et Ouest
North and West Façades

Fassaden nord und west
Facciata nord e ponente
Fachadas norte e ponente

Fachada principal iluminada
Façade principale illuminée
Main façade illuminated

Beleuchtete Hauptfassade
Facciata principale illuminato
Fachada principal iluminada

Monasterio: Fachada del mediodía con la Galería de Convalecientes y la alberca
Le Monastère: Façade sud, Galerie des Convalescents et pièce d´eau
Monastery: South façade with the Galería de Convalescents and the reservoir

Kloster: Suedfassade mit der Galeríe der Genesender und Zisterne
Monastero: Facciata di mezzogiorno con la Galleria dei Convalescenti e il laghetto
Mosteiro: Fachada do meio-dia com a Galaria dos Convalescentes e a alverca

Monasterio iluminado
Le Monastère illuminé
Illuminated Monastery

Aufgeklärt Kloster
Monastero illuminato
Mosteiro iluminado

Patio de los Reyes
Cour des Rois
Court of the Kings

Hof der Koenig
Cortile dei Re
Pátio dos Reis

Silla de Felipe II
Chaise de Philippe II
Philip II´s Seat

Stuhl des Filip II
Sedia di Filippo II
Cadeira de Felipe II

The five arches of the facade lead to a porch or vaulted vestibule 38 metres long by 5 metres wide. The exterior arches have a corresponding number of interior ones, all with doors; the three central ones lead into the church, and of these the side ones display beneath the arch large black marble medallions with Latin inscriptions in gilded bronze letters. The first inscription alludes to the laying of the first stone of the temple by the founder King on St. Bernard's Day (the 20th of August, 1563) and the commencement of the divine offices on the eve feast day of San Lorenzo (the 9th of August, 1586), and the second to the consecration of the Basilica (30th of August, 1595).

On entering through any of these three doors (whose framework is of the finest acana wood from the Antilles, and whose panelling is in oak), one goes into the church through the temple *Atrio* (portal) or *lower choir*, which is nearly 17 metres square; four square pillars form a transept at the ends of which are four large arches with as many doors (the entrance one, the two side ones which lead to the "patinejos" (little patios) and the front one which leads into the church). There are also four little chapels formed from their angles: the two beside the entrance serve as screens and the other two are dedicated to Saints Cosmas and Damian and to Saints Blase and Sixtus respectively. The pillars support a splendid vault which, in the words of Father Quevedo, "in spite of its large fugue it appears to be as level as the pavement and even somewhat convex in shape". It is because of this optical illusion that it is commonly known as the *"flat vaulting"*.

Passing through these chapels in the direction of the temple we come to the *Seminary's Choir*, three spaces of 5 metres in length by 3,90 in width, surrounded by walnut seats where, in days gone by, the seminarists used to sing Mass at dawn.

The Temple

One enters the temple through the Seminary's Choir by
a large door with a bronze grating which was cast and gilded
in Zaragoza in the workshop of Tujaron. A further four doors
with similar gratings by the same craftsman correspond to the
main one. The church is in the shape of a square with sides
some 50 metres in length and its architecture is Doric, imitating the style of Saint Peter's in Rome **(p. 38-39);** four
enormous central pillars support, on squinches, the gigantic
cupola (92 metres in height from the ground) and together with a
further eight opposite them, projecting from the walls, they form
the props for 24 arches which support the vaults. These divi-
sions create the plan of a Greek cross with the three naves forming its arms. In the central pillars, and in the part which faces
the minor naves, there are two openings in the wall which are
finished with high, pointed arches; in the lower, there are
large altars; in the upper part there is a tribune with its gilded
bronze railing without any means of access. The altars and tribune form the eight mural pillars. A gallery with a bronze balustrade runs round the whole church at a height of some 8,50
metres. There are 38 windows which shed light into the temple,
of which eight belong to the dome. The brick vaultings are
covered outside by lead plate, and inside they were originally
stuccoed, except those which belong to the main altar and to
the choir, which were painted by Lucas Cambiasso, Luchetto.
In the reing of Charles II the stuccoes were removed and were
painted equally in fresco work by Lucas Jordán; the subjects
depicted in these vaultings starting from the altar of the
Annunciation (Gospel side) are as follows: 1st. *The Mystery*

of the Incarnation; 2nd. *The Israelites crossing the Desert and the Red Sea;* 3rd. *Triumph of the Church Militant;* 4th. *Resurrection of the Flesh;* 5th. *Purity of the Virgin;* 6th. *Victory of the Israelites over the Amalekites;* 7th. *The Judgement of Saint Hieronymous* and 8th. *The Death, Burial and Assumption of the Virgin;* in the four squinches are *Saints Ambrose, Augustin* and *Gregory,* Doctors of the Church; and the emblems of *Saint Hieronymous, the lion guarding his mantle and cardinale.*

Finally, the church is paved in white marble brought from the Sierra de los Filabres (Granada) and grey marble from Estremoz (Alemtejo), Portugal.

Before passing on to the description of the main Chapel with its great retable and royal tombs, the most important part of the temple on account of its treasures, we should notice the paintings which belong to the other altars of the Basilica, 43 in all, situated in the hollows of the recesses, as has already been mentioned, on the pillars, the walls and the chapels. These oil paintings have simple, golden, rectangular frames and circular frontispieces in a white, marble-like paste by José Marzal in 1829.

The altar pictures are arranged in such a way as to show pairs of Saints, both male and female, from the major litanies, bearing their attributes: it can be seen that they follow a plan which must have originated from the architect Juan de Herrera, and ultimately from the King himself. These canvases belong to a group of Spanish painters, among whom the most notable are Juan Fernández de Navarrete, el Mudo (1526-1579) who composed a striking Apostleship in six canvases with an impressive Spanish expression; Alonso Sánchez Coello (1531-2, -1588) and Luis Carvajal, and in the second row Diego Urbina and the brothers Martín and Juan Gómez, the last of these being the most famous. The group of Italian painters which

intervened subsequent and successively were Rómulo Cincinato, Lucas Cambiasso, Luchetto, Federico Zúccaro and Peregrín of Peregrini or Tibaldi, who painted their compositions in
a series depicting the development of the life of a Saint.

The altar tables are made from granite and grey marble.
In 1963, an important and very appropriate electrical installation was completed in these altars as well as in the remainder
of the church (the Main Chapel, vaults, choir) and, in this way,
the paintings can be appreciated in all their beauty.

Starting from the pulpit on the Gospel side, the altars,
their paintings and their images come in the following order:

1. *Saints Peter and Paul,* by Juan Fernández de Navarrete,
"el Mudo".

2. In front: *Saints Philip and James,* by the same, completed by Diego de Urbina.

3. Altar of Relics: *The Annunciation,* by Federico Zúccaro,
renovated by Juan Gómez. **(P. 116-117).**

4. Chapel: *Saint Ann,* by Lucas Cambiasso, Luchetto.

5. Chapel: *St. John the Baptist preaching in the Desert,*
by Luchetto (in the passage of this chapel Queen Doña María
de las Mercedes, first wife of Alphonso XII, is buried).

6. *St. John the Evangelist and St. Matthew,* by Navarrete,
"el Mudo".

7. In front: *Saints Mark and Luke,* by the same.

8. Chapel: *St. Ildephonse and St. Eugene,* Archbishops of
Toledo, by Luis de Carvajal.

9. Chapel: *St. Michael contending against the bad Angels,*
by Peregrín Tibaldi.

10. *St. Isidore and St. Leander,* brothers, Archbishops of
Seville, by Carvajal.

11. *Saints Fabian and Sebastian,* by Diego de Urbina.

12.   In front: *The holy children Justo and Pastor,* by Alonso Sánchez Coello.

13.   Chapel: *Martyrdom of St. Maurice and the Theban Legion,* by Rómulo Cincinato; it was for this place that El Greco painted his picture on the same subject, which is preserved in the Salas Capitulares because Philip II was not very pleased with the excessively personal interpretation of this artist. Today it is exhibited in the Room of Honor of the New Museum of Paintings; it has always held an outstanding place among the best paintings of El Escorial.

14.   Chapel: *Saints Ambrose and Gregory,* Pope, by Diego de Urbina.

15.   *Saint Theresa of Avila,* by Domingo Fierros, 1879, which substitutes the original painting for this place which was *Saint Gregory Nazianzen and Saint John Chrysostom* by Luis de Carvajal, now in another part of the Monastery.

16.   Chapel: *Saint Basil and Saint Athanasius,* by Alonso Sánchez Coello.

17.   In front: *Saint Bonaventure and Saint Thomas Aquinas,* by Carvajal.

18.   Chapel: *Saint Hieronymous and Saint Augustin,* by Sánchez Coello.

19.   Chapel: Altar with a carved image of *Our Lady of Consolation,* Patroness of the Order of Saint Augustin. The painting described next was originally in this Chapel.

20.   *Saint Paul, the Hermit and Saint Anthony, the Abbot,* by Sánchez Coello.

21.   *Saint Lawrence and Saint Stephen,* martyrs, by the same.

22.   Beneath the Choir: *Saint Sixtus,* Pope *and Saint Blase,* bishop, by Carvajal.

23. Beneath the Choir: *Saints Cosmas and Damian,* by the same; drawing by Navarrete, "el Mudo".

24. *Saint Martha and Saint Mary Magdalen,* by Diego de Urbina.

25. In front: *Saints Vincent and George,* by Sánchez Coello.

26. Chapel: Altar and carved image of *Our Lady of Protection.*

27. Chapel: *Saints Leocadia and Engracia,* martyrs, by Carvajal.

28. *Saints Clare and Scholastica,* by Diego de Urbina.

29. *Saints Agatha and Lucy* by the same.

30. *Saints Cecile and Barbara,* martyrs, by Carvajal.

31. Chapel: *Saints Paula and Monique,* widows, by Diego de Urbina.

32. Chapel: *Saints Catherine and Agnes,* martyrs, by Sánchez Coello.

33. Chapel: *Altar of the Cristo de la Buena Muerte;* carved life-size crucifix.

34. *Saints Martin and Nicholas,* Bishops, by Carvajal.

35. In front: *St. Anthony of Padua and St. Peter of Verona,* martyr, by the same.

36. Chapel: *Saints Dominic and Francis of Assisi,* by the same.

37. Chapel: *Martyrdom of Saint Ursula and Companions, the eleven thousand virgins:* sketched by Peregrín Tibaldi and executed by Juan Gómez. The beautiful white marble sculpture called *Cellini's Christ* has now been installed here. The cross is made of black marble from Carrara, encrusted in another one in order to fasten it more safely; under Christ's feet there is a Latin inscription which translated reads as follows: *Benvenuto Cellini, Florentine citizen, made it in 1562.* The size os the Saviour's body is supposed to be the real one,

according to the measurements of the Holy Sheet which is kept
in Turin. The sculpture is a work of art, specially the head,
and its value increases as it is the only known Christ by
Benvenuto.

38. *St. Benedict and St. Bernard*, Abbots, by A. Sánchez
Coello.

39. *St. Bartholomew and St. Thomas*, Apostles, by J. Fernández Navarrete, "el Mudo".

40. In front: *St. Barnabas and St. Matthew*, Apostles, by
the same.

41. Altar of Relics: *Saint Hieronymous in the Desert*, by
Federico Zúccaro, renovated by Navarrete, "el Mudo".

42. *St. James and St. Andrew*, Apostles, by "el Mudo".

43. In front: *Saints Simon and Jude*, Apostles, by the
same.

Main Chapel and retable, pulpits and lamps

The Main Chapel is a continuation of the central nave
of the temple **(p. 38-39)**; it measures some 20 metres
long by 15 wide, and is separated from the nave by a large
arch on pilasters and on a level with the ground, by 12 steps
of blood-red marble brought from Espeja (Soria). At the end of
the staircase is the Presidente or Chancel, the floor of which
is paved with white, green and red marble and jasper, which
are combined to form beautiful patterns. On each side of this
platform are the Oratories and Royal Tombs; five further steps
lead down to a second platform decorated with gilded bronze
handrails, and on this platform, raised upon two more steps,
is the Main Altar (3,50 metres wide by 1,40 deep), also

fashioned from beautifully combined marble and jasper and completely independent for its better service. The altar slab is fashioned from a single piece of fine jasper, and it covers the entire altar. On both sides, against the wall, there are two seats with backs made from fine woods.

The shole of the back of the Chapel has a large socle almost three metres high with a frieze and cornice, fashioned from blood-red marble with parts of it made from green jasper from the Sierra Nevada; on the right and left hand sides of the altar, and in this socle, there are two beautiful doors with door-jambs and lintels also made from green jasper; on the inside they are made of mahogany, and on the side that faces the temple, they are covered with jasper mosaics of different colours, with their frames and mouldings made of gilded bronze. These are the two doors which lead to the Sacrarium, and the other two give access one to the Palace, and the other to Philip II's rooms. The *Sacrarium* is built with a 1,40 metres arch the back of which is open in the wall behind the centre of the first structure of the retable, which is reached from the doors by two marble staircases of eleven steps and two landings. The upper one leads to the Tabernacle, and the walls are covered with red marble and white inlaid work as far as the second landing, and in the remainder, up to the turn of the arch, which appears like a rainbow, are depicted four stories from the Old Testament which refer to the Mystery of the Eucharist: *Abraham offering the tithes of victory to Melchizedek; the Israelites gathering manna; the Legal Supper and Elias receiving from the hands of the angel "bread baked under ashes"*, painted as a fresco by Peregrín Tibaldi. Upon this large Chapel socle rests the Main Retable **(p. 38-39-40)** after the very beautiful classical plan of Juan de Herrera, one of the most notable works of the Monastery because of its

Fachada de Oriente
Façade Est
East façade

Ostfassade
Facciata d´oriente
Fachada do oriente

Vista exterior con una de las torres
Vue extérieure avec l´une des tours
Outside view with one of the towers

Aeussere Ansicht mit einem von den Tuermen
Vista esterna con una delle torri
Vista exterior com uma das torres

Patio de los Evangelistas
Cour des Evangélistes
Court of the Evangelists

Hof der Evangelisten
Cortile degli Evangelisti
Pátio dos Evangelistas

Vista nocturna iluminada de la fachada meridional del Monasterio
Façade sud du Monastère; la nuit, avec illumination
Night view of the illuminated southern façade of the Monastery

Nachtsanblick auf dei Suedfassade des klosters in Licht
Vista notturna illuminata della facciata meridionale del Monastero
Vista noturna iluminada da fachada meridional do Mosteiro

Nave central. Bóveda pintada por Lucas Cambiasso
Nef centrale. Voûte peinte par Lucas Cambiasso
Central nave. Arched roof painted by Lucas Cambiasso

Mittelschiff. Gewoelbe bemahll von Lucas Cambiasso
Navata centrale. Volta dipinta da Lucas Cambiasso
Nave central. Abóbeda pintada por Lucas Cambiasso

Nave central con el altar mayor
La nef avec le maître-autel
Central nave with High Altar

Mittelschiff mit dem Hochaltar
Navata centrale con l'Altare Maggiore
Nave central com o Altar Maior

Grupo orante de Felipe II. Tabernáculo
Groupe orant de Philippe II. Tabernacle
Group at prayer formed by Philip II. Tabernacle

Betende Gruppe mit Filip II. Tabernakel
Gruppo orante di Filippo II. Tabernacolo
Grupo orante de Felípe II. Tabernáculo

artistic value and richness. Its measurements are unusual, but harmonious, (14 metres wide by 26 high), because of the admirable distribution of the huge surface in four structures or horizontal zones, divided up by columns in the Roman style, that is to say, superimposing the styles of each one: Doric in the first, or lower zone; Ionic in the second; Corinthian in the third and Composite in the fourth, with their respective entablatures. In the architectonic, it is constructed with red marble and green jasper, using fine varieties of the latter and other brilliant colours to emphasize the decorative details. All the bases, capitals and adornments of the altar are of gilded bronze.

The work was contracted in 1579 and the Leonis, bronze sculptors of Milano, were to make all the statues which appear in the retable, fifteen in all; Juan Bautista Comane was to work with the marbles. When this last one died, he was succeeded by his brother Pedro Castello who finished and polished the jasper columns, finishing an excellent work in 1594. He was then considered sculptor to the King. **(P. 56)**.

The first structure or lower zone is Doric style, as indicated, and it rests upon a base of six red marble columns of 70 cm. in diametre and 5 metres high, with its corresponding architrave, which originate five compartments: the center one is occupied by the Tabernacle and on its sides, two paintings by Peregrín Tibaldi: *The Adoration of the Shepherds* and *The Adoration of the Kings,* the exterior compartments present two superimposed niches in green jasper, with life size gilded bronze statues (by León and Pompeyo Leoni, as well as all the others located in the Retable), which represent the four Doctors of the Church: *St. Hieronymous, St. Augustine, St. Ambrose and St. Gregory,* "worked with admirable delicateness and fineness."

The second zone or structure, Ionic style, is arranged similarly. The paintings, which are three now, occupy the central spaces and represent *The martyrdom of St. Lawrence* (center) by Tibaldi, and on each side, *Scourging at the Pillar* and *Christ carrying the Cross.* by Federico Zúccaro. In the extremes and in their corresponding superimposed niches are statues of the *Four Evangelists,* somewhat larger than life size.

The third zone, Corinthian style, has only four columns and in the three spaces between them there are three oil-paintings by Zúccaro: *The Assumption of the Virgin* and on the sides, *The Resurrection of Our Lord* and *the Descent of the Holy Ghost.* In the extremes there are two statues, also somewhat larger than life size, of the Apostles *St. Andrew* and *St. James.*

The final structure, the Composite one, has only two columns between which is formed a chapel with a most beautiful *Calvary. Christ hanging upon the Cross, with the Virgin and St. John* on either side, a work of moving pathetic realism. At the ends, the statues of *St. Peter and St. Paul,* larger than life-size, like the rest of the statues in this group, which finishes with a triangular frontispiece of the same red marble, touching the key-stone of the dome at the foot of the statue of *St. Paul.* Here we find the signature of *Pompeious Leoni (fecit) 1588* **(p. 49).**

The whole of the sculpture work in the retable, together with the royal burial groups, constitute the masterpieces of those Milanese bronze sculptors, Pompei Leoni and his father, León Leoni, who rose to fame mainly because of the many commissions they received for El Escorial.

On the other hand, the collection of paintings cannot be qualified in quite the same way; they are merely creditable and beautiful.

The *Tabernacle* also constitutes a unique jewel in the ensemble of the Main Retable; it is the most perfect and richest of its kind which has ever been made. It is situated beneath the arch which is formed in the central intercolumniation of the first structure of the altar; it is 4,50 metres in height and 2 metres in diameter. Its invention and design are to be attributed to Juan de Herrera and it was fashioned by Jacome Trezzo, a craftsman in the service of Philip II for many years, "who invented many useful tools and machines which enabled him to work with the skill which is evident, but, with all, he took 7 years to complete it". It was committed to his charge in 1579.

It forms a small circular temple, Corinthian in style, with fine marble, jasper and bronze for all the decorative details; a jasper socle supports eight equidistant columns, also of red jasper veined with white from Aracena (Huelva), very beautiful, but so hard that the craftsman had to use diamonds to shape them; these columns support the same number of gilded bronze statuettes of the Apostles, 28 cm. in height which, with four others gathered in the recesses of the intercolumniations, complete the Twelve Apostles. From the podium in which the pedestals are secured, the cupola begins, and is crowned by a lantern with its little cupola, complete with the figure of the Saviour, made from the same material and of the same size as the other statuettes. Inside, a structure or cylindrical box is attached to the columns forming as it were the wall of the Tabernacle with mouldings, recesses and doors, the latter with bronze ornamentations and frontispieces. Four doors correspond to the four cardinal points and the remaining four intercolumniations form four closed recesses where four statues of the Apostles are situated **(p. 40).**

The Tabernacle was taken to pieces during the French invasion and was restored, by order of Ferdinand VII by Manuel de

Urquiza in 1827, as we are told by a Latin inscription set in the right or east door. The magnificent interior pyx was of pure gold and precious stones with "a topaze as large as a fist" hanging from the vault of the Tabernacle, but they all disappeared during the Napoleonic invasion. In the lower socle of the Tabernacle there is a Latin inscription written by the Humanist Benito Arias Montano, so fond of the King, which, when translated, reads "King Philip II dedicated this work to Jesus Christ, Priest and Victim; it is made completely from Spanish marble, and was accomplished by Jacobo de Trezzo from Milan".

Oratories and Royal Monuments

The Oratories and Royal Monuments complement in a solemn and admirable fashion the magnificence of the Main Altar and the Tabernacle.

On both sides of the first landing of the Chapel there are great arches, 8 metres wide, in the recesses of which are the Royal monuments and oratories, forming a Doric architectural structure, divided in two parts. A 3 metres high socle occupies the entire width of the 8 metres arch, in which there are three doors with their frames of green marble from Sierra Nevada, jasper panelling and bronze ornamentation. The doors nearest to the gradatories lead to the Sacristy and reliquaries; the other two lead to the oratories, on both sides of which are two chapels of beautiful and variously combined marble where the Royal personages heard Mass. The one on the Epistle side corresponds to the alcove where Philip II dies **(fig. 9)**.

These oratories form the pedestal or socle for the burials which occupy the second structure like a chapel or a deep tribune 3 metres deep by 4 metres high which fills the entire width of the arch. The outer Doric columns and pilasters correspond to other interior pilasters and the walls between them and those of the sides are covered with Black marble from Miranda de Ebro. They are adorned with Latin inscriptions in gilded bronze which lettering refers to the royal personages represented in each of the groups which occupy the central intercolumniations of both chaplets; the groups comprise five praying figures, larger than life-size and fashioned in gilded copper or brass (p. 49-54).

On the Gospel side is that of the Emperor and his family (p. 50-51). The first and principal figure is that of Charles V, wearing armour and with his imperial cloak on which the two headed eagle in black marble from Mérida stands out. The Emperor's head is bared, his hands are joined in an attitude of prayer, like those of all the figures in both groups, and he is kneeling on a large cushion in front of a prayer-desk covered in rich brocade, all in gilded bronze. On his right is the Empress Elizabeth, his wife, mother of Philip II; behind is his daughter María who married Maximilian II of Austria, both similarly dressed in cloaks with the imperial eagle, and further behind are the Emperor's sisters: María, Queen of Hungary and Leonor, Queen of France, all kneeling. This structure is completed with a Doric architrave, and on top of it is yet another, Ionic, with two columns which flank the great imperial crest bearing the two-headed eagle and the Golden Fleece, all in marble with the colours combined in such a way as to indicate accurately the heraldic colours. The other details are in gilded bronze, like the capitals, bases and other accessories which belong to the ensemble; the section is completed with an architrave and a frontispiece.

The monument on the Epistle side is exactly the same. In the central intercolumniation there are a further five lifesize bronze statues, all with their heads bared and kneeling in an attitude of prayer **(p. 54–55)**. The first is Philip II wearing a mantle encrusted with the royal crest, fahioned in mosaics and marble of different colours, an extremely skilful piece of work. In front of him is a prayer-desk, draped in a rich brocade; on his right is Queen Anne, his fourth wife and mother of Philip III; behind is Isabel de Valois, who was his third wife; beside her is María of Portugal, his first wife, and mother of Prince Charles, who is depicted behind her. This chapel is completed in the same way as the opposite one, but the coat-of-arms, which is that of Philip II, is more accurately executed. The inscriptions above the facings are also similar to their twin but the name on this side is that of Philip II. These groups of figures are without doubt the masterpieces of Pompeyo Leoni; the appropriateness of the postures, the nobility and gracefulness of the figures, the absolute realism, the elegance of the whole group, the richness and sumptuous ornamentation of their vesture, the entire composition with the unfailing tact in the placing of the figures, constitutes one of the most vividly lasting impressions implanted in the memory of the visitors to the Monastery.

Finally, the vault of the Main Chapel is painted in fresco work by Luchetto who depicted there in the *Coronation of the Virgin* and the *Four Major Prophets* beside the windows.

Further pieces of interest are the *Pulpits,* the Lamps and the Reliquaries; there are two pulpits, situated on the first step as one ascends to the Main Altar; their style is completely different from that of the time when the Monastery was founded, for they use marble tablets which came from the Monastery of Parraces (Segovia), a work executed by Manuel de Urquiza, bronze sculptor to the King, commissioned by Ferdinand VII until 1827. They are made of marble, with columns, handrails and ornaments in gilded bronze; the one on the right hand side (Epistle) has some medallions with the four doctors of the Church and the arms of the Monastery; the one on the left (Gospel) has the four Evangelists and the royal coat-of-arms; the gilded sounding-board are supported by four small columns complete with cupolas on top of which are the statues of Faith and Religion.

In the Church, there are two large, beautiful *chandeliers* made of gilded bronze: *El Clavel* (carnation) made by Juan Simón in 1571; and The *Tenebrario* of the same style and making. The gilded bronze lamp, in the style of the Empire, hangs before the Main Chapel and serves to illuminate the Sacrament; it was fashioned in about 1833 by the silversmiths from Madrid, Nicolás Cervantes and Manuel García.

The *Reliquaries,* or relics' altars, are also two in number and occupy the eastern fore parts of the minor naves; they have doors of two foliations which serve as retables for the altars of the *Annunciation* and of *St. Hieronymous.* In the seven shelves, there are kept various types and forms of relics; shrines, lanterns, boxes, little chests, arms and heads, for the most par in gilded bronze, fashioned in Seville during the reign of Philip III. The material wealth was very great, but the Napoleonic invasion changed all this; its richness in relics is still very great.

There are two other chapels, 8 metres in height, situated above the former Reliquaries. They seem to be retables of wood with paintings of various Saints on the inside and the outside of the doors. The paintings above the Relicario of St. Hieronymous are by Martín Gómez, and those which belong to the Altar of the Ascension are by Bartolomé Carducho.

The staircase known as *Patrocinio* leads from the Church up to the Choir and begins near the door of the Pantheons. At the end of it, there are two corridors or transits around the Temple.

One follows the Southern lateral nave, and the other one corresponds with this one on the northern side or Palace. Some paintings by Miguel Coxcie are displayed in them including *Jesus Christ and the Virgin interceding for the World before the Eternal Father;* by Fray Nicolás Borrás there is *St. Hieronymous praying;* and by Navarrete el Mudo there is the *Call to the Apostolate of Saint Peter and Saint Andrew.*

Antechoirs

These are two spacious halls, 6,50 metres by 17 metres which extend from North to South along the sides of the Choir. The floors are paved with white and grey marble. The vaultings, divided up by four lunettes, have four stories of David painted in fresco by Lucas Jordán: *the Prophet Nathaniel reprimands him for adultery and homicide; the Prophet Gaad gives him a choice between hunger, war and plague (in front); David offers sacrifices of atonement to the Lord; David intonates praise of the Lord to the sound of his lyre.* There are two large doors in this western antechoir which lead to the main high Cloister, and between them there is a small chapel made of grey marble with jasper mosaic, and a holy-water font; above this, in the higher part, there is a recess with an Italian statue in white marble which represents *San Lorenzo.*

The Antechoir of the College section is similar to the former, but in the northern fore-part there is only one little door which leads to a fountain with its little facade fashioned from grey marble. The vaulting, also painted by Jordán, depicts four stories of Salomon: *the priest Sadoc and the Prophet Nathaniel consecrate him King of Israel; he has a dream in which the Lord inspires him with wisdom; the Judgement of Salomon; the*

Remate del altar mayor. Calvario
Partie supérieure du maître-autel. Calvaire
Top of the High Altar. Calvary

Gipfel des Hochaltars. Kalvarienberg
Termine dell´Altare Maggiore. Calvario
Remate do altar maior. Calvário

49

D · O · M

CAROLO · V · ROM · IMPERAT · AVG
HOR · REGN · VTR · SICIL · ET · HIER · R
ARCHID · AVSTRIÆ · OPTIM · PARE
PHILIPPVS · FILIVS · P

IACENT · SIMVL · ELISABETHA · VX
ET · MARIA · FILIA · IMPERATRIC
ELEONORA · ET · MARIA · SOROR
ILLA · FRANC · HÆC · HVNGAR · REG

HVNC · LOCVM · QVIS · POSTEROR · CAR
V · AVITAM · GLOR · RER · GESTAR · SPLEN
DORE · SVPERAVERIS · IPSE · SOLVS
OCCVPATO · CÆTERI · REVERENTER
ABSTINETE

HIDA · POSTERITA
BERVM · NEPOTVM · Q
ASVM · RELICTVS · LOC
GAM · ANNORVM · SE
CVM · NATVRÆ · PERS
OCCVPANDVS

Cenotafio del Emperador Carlos V
Cénotaphe de l'Empereur Charles V
Cenotaph of the Emperor Charles V

Das Grabdenkmal Kaiser Karls V
Cenotáfio dell'Imperatore Carlo V
Cenotáfio do Imperador Carlos V

Coro alto, con los órganos y el facistol; al fondo el retablo mayor
Le chœur supérieur, avec les orgues et le lutrin; au fond le grand rétable
High Choir with organs and lectern; in the background the Main Retable

Obere Chor, mit den Orgeln und Chorpult; im Grunde Hauptaltarblatt
Coro alto, con gli organi e il leggio; al fondo la pala maggiore
Côro alto, com os orgaos e o facistol; ao fondo o retábulo maior

HIC·LOCVS·DIGNIORI·INTER
POSTEROS·ILLO·QVI·VELRO·AB
EO·ABSTINVIT·VIRTVTIS·ERGO
ASSERVATVR·ALITER·IMMVNIS
ESTO

D·O·M
HILIPPVS·II·OMNIVM·HISPAN.
GNOR·VTR·SICIL·ET·HIERVS.
CATHOL·ARCHIDVX·AVSTR.
HAC·SACRA·AEDE·QAM·A·FVND.
EXTRVXIT·SIBI·VIVENS·P.

QVIESCVNT·SIMVL·ANNA
ABETHA·ET·MARIA·VXORES
·CAROLO·PRINC·FIL·PRIMOG.

LIBERORVM·STVDIO
POST·DIVTINA·SPATIA
DESIGNATVS·LOCV
QVVM·NATVRAE·CO
NT·MONVMENTI
·CORANDVS

Cenotafio de Felipe II
Cénotaphe de Philippe II
Cenotaph of Philip II

Das Grabdenkmal Philipps II
Cenotafio del Re Filippo II
Cenotáfio de Filipe II

Altar Mayor   Der Hochaltar
Maître-autel   Altare Maggiore
High Altar   Altar maior

*Queen of Sheba marvels at the wisdom with which Salomon
explains the enigmas which she presents to him.* Part of the
walls of both are occupied by shelving and the books of the
Choir.

The Choir

The Choir is entered through two large arches in which the
antechoirs finish, and it is situated above the entrance to the
Church at a height of eight metres **(p. 52-53).** There is a
range of bronze balconies which close it in the temple section.
The pavement is made of white and grey marble, just like that
of the Antechoir. The Choir is 14 metres wide, 27 long, and
measures 23 in height up to the keystone of the vault. Various
windows, which look our over the Patio de los Reyes (Courtyard of the Kings) shed light upon it. In the sides and fore-
part are situated the *Stalls,* which consist of two levels of seats,
upper and lower, the former separated from the latter by a platform of two metres. Its architecture is in the Corinthian style.
It was designed by Juan de Herrera, and executed by the
Italian cabinet-maker Giuseppe Flecha, and, under his direction,
by the Spanish Maestros: Gamboa, Quesada, Serrano and
Aguirre, who worked in beautifully inlaid fine woods (acana,
mahogany, ebony, terebinth, cedar, box-wood and walnut). The
upper seats are similar to the lower ones except for their
extended backing from which rise columns which support a
cornice and its decorations, forming a canopy which completes
the stalls at a height of four metres, and elegantly emphasizes
the work. The carving is exquisite. The prior's seat is in the
middle of the western forefront, beautifully executed in the
same Corinthian style, with 16 columns (8 of which rise up on
the prior's seat and a further 4 on each of its sides) with its

tympan and its vault. Another small block or chaplet with four compound pillars is raised above this structure, and in the intercolumniations there is a painting on linen which depicts the head and shoulders of the *Saviour,* (from the 16th Century Italian School), This block is completed with a frontispiece in which there stands a small statue of San Lorenzo on a pedestal with a gridiron and a book. In both choirs, there is a total of 124 seats, and the one on the end, in the right angle made by the front with the southern fore-part, is the one which Philip II always occupied when he assisted at the Divine Office in this Choir. It is somewhat wider than the others and beside it there is a little door through which the King came and went out and received messages without hindering or distracting the Community.

Organs and Paintings

In the middle of the two-side walls of the Choir there are two great organs in the upper stalls, facing each other, and these are supported by two balconies with a gilded bronze railing where the singers were situated. The organ cases are in Corinthian style, made from pinewood of Cuenca, very well gilded, 5.600 metres in width and with a proportionate height, and these reach up to the cornice which runs around the temple. These two, with two other larger ones which were situated on both sides of the transept of the Church, were four great organs which the Basilica of El Escorial had, and to which were added four other small portable ones. Philip II commissioned them to be constructed by the most famous European organ builder, maese Gil Brevost, who died during the work and was succeeded by his sons who achieved the same expertness and fame as their father. The smaller ones have disappeared. The two in the transept retain only their beautiful cases, and were perfectly restored in 1963. Those of the Choir were reconstructed in 1930 and, among the many restorations which were completed for the fourth centenary of the foundation of the Monastery, they were also perfected in 1963. The console for playing them is situated in the middle of the Choir.

, At the sides of the organs of the choir there are four large pictures (two on each side), drawn by Luchetto and finished by Rómulo Cincinato, with fashioned frames, and they depict two episodes in the life of San Lorenzo; *The Saint goes out to meet Pope St. Sixtus when the latter is being led out to martyrdom,* and *the Saint presents the Prefect of Rome with a multitude of poor people as true treasures of the Christian Church, instead of the material treasure for which he had been requested* (south side); and in front, (north side) two more episodes in the life of St. Hieronymous; *the Saint writes his commentaries on the Bible, and an angel sounds a trumpet in his ear,* an allusion to how he held as everpresent the Last Judgement. In the background he can be seen doing his penance; *St. Hieronymous explains the rule to this monks;* in the distance can be seen his burial.

Between the windows of the fore-part beneath the cornice, there are the large figures of *San Lorenzo* and *Saint Hieronymous,* and in the middle of the fore-part, above, the cornice, there is the *Annunciation,* in which the Virgin remains on one side of the large window, and the Angel on the other. On each side of this fore-part there are two balconies and over them there are two recesses, at the back of which are depicted the matron figures of *The Faith* and *The Church* (south) and *Prudence* and *Justice* (north). Above the two arches through which one enters the Choir, there are a further number of rectangular recesses in which are depicted standing in pairs, larger than life-size, *Charity* and *Hope* in one, and *Fortitude* and *Temperance* in the other. This entire collection of figures (except for the pictures) are the work of Lucas Cambiasso, Luchetto.

By the same artist is the painting on the *vault* in which a representation of *Glory* fills the entire space. Towards the forepart there is the Blessed Trinity on a throne of light, surrounded by Cherubims and celestial spirits; on the right of Jesus Christ is His Blessed Mother, and then the Choir of Apostles, among whom St. John stands out; for the rest, there are Choirs of Angels and Saints of all states and conditions, who are identified by their habits, instruments of their martyrdom or their insignias, and these are distributed in zones or bands. At the entrance of *Glory,* on the northern side over the left cornice, Luchetto put the portrait of *Fr. Antonio de Villacastín,* a lay brother of the Monastery of San Lorenzo, an overseer of its construction, and also his own portrait. It is somewhat unfortunate that the personages are arranged in parallel series, seated as though in an amphitheatre, as this results in a rather monotonous composition.

Chandelier and Lectern

From an enormous 20 metres bar of iron, that weighs 345 kilograms, there hangs from the centre of the vault a magnificent chandelier of rock crystal formed by four peacocks whose extended tails unite in the centre and finish, in the upper part, in an eagle on a half globe. Little flower vases, pendents and other ornaments form the sockets for 27 lights. It was fashioned in Milan, acquired by the Marquis of Astorga who wanted to present it to the king, Charles II, who in turn donated it to the Monastery in 1676. It is badly damages, for during the Napoleonic invasion, many French troops removed a number of its ornaments and pendents.

Another notable piece is the huge lectern. It is situated at the entrance to the Choir, in front of the seats, in the central axis of the room; on a square socle 21 cms. in height, and made from blood-red jasper with white marble compartments, are situated four gilded bronze pilasters and upon these rest various thick bars of iron which, joined to the tree, or interior axis, serve to move the magnificent lectern. Its structure is shaped like a truncated pyramid which ends in a cornice. Above this cornice there are four bronze globes and, as a finishing touch, it has a beautiful templet upon a pedestal shaped like a Greek cross from whose ends and twelve little fluted columns (four on each side) originate four facades with their triangular frontispieces, between which is raised the little cupola finished with a cross. The templet is made of rich woods with bronze adornments. In the interior there stands a statuette of the Virgin which is said to be attributed to Luisa Roldán.

The shelves in the lectern are made from acana from the Antilles with stripes of gilt bronze, just like the edgings where the hymn books rest. Its widest periphery amounts to 11 metres, 2,80 metres per pilaster, and that same distance up to the cornice. The total height of the enormous lectern is 4,50 metres.

The Library of the Choir

The Choir Library is located in the antechoirs and is a spacious room 22 metres by 7 metres wide, behind the antechoir on the convent side. Against the walls are the cases made

from the same fine woods as the choir, but oak was abundantly
used here because it resists the great weight and the conti-
nuous friction made by the sliding of the books. It is the work
of Flecha and his Spanish assistants, who also made the choir
stalls. It follows the Doric style.

On August 8, 1586, the first books were shelved there
"which are undoubtedly of a greatness unequalled in the
world". The collection consists of 216 choral books which,
because of their exquisite caligraphy and the beauty of their
illuminations, make up the last original chapter in Spanish
miniature work. The workshop of El Escorial represents the
most exact and exuberant manifestation of the Renaissance in
the art of books "incoporating the great painting of the most
famous Italian Maestros (Leonardo, Rafael, Miguel Angel), to
the illustration of the manuscript books". All these choral
books are written with singular beauty, exquisiteness and
care on beautiful uniform white male goat and kid parchment.
Each of the pages containing chants has four lines and those
which do not contain music have 10; the form and writing is
the same for all the books, which, when opened, measure 1,67
metres wide by 1,12 high. The binding, too, is uniform, made
from sturdy boards covered with natural colour cowhide, protected and adorned with five nails or bosses, corner plates and
clasps all of gilded bronze. Each volume slides over two wheels.
They were bound by the Flemish Peter Bosch.

The illuminations were executed by Fr. Andrés de León,
lay brother of the Monastery, his disciple Fr. Julián de la Fuente el Saz, another lay brother (the *Breviary* of 1568 and the
Capitulary are the work of both artists) and Ambrosio Salazar
(the three *Pasionarios* and the *Office of Santiago* are done by
Fr. Julián and the beginning of the *Mass of St. Simon and
St. Judas* is by Salazar). The writers or caligraphers were

Cristóbal Ramírez, a native of Valencia; Fr. Martín de Palencia, a Benedictine monk from Valladolid; Francisco Hernández, who lived in Segovia; Pedro Jaloverte, who lived in Burgos, and, from 1781, Pedro Gómez, who lived in Cuenca.

Cornices and dome

Beneath the arches which lead to the choir from the ante-choirs, a door on the convent side leads through a corridor and staircases up to the organ, and from there another corridor is divided into two. The one on the left leads to the bell tower and the other on the right leads to what is commonly called the Cornices, which is a corridor opened into the thickness of the wall, through which one can walk around the temple at the height of the projecting cornice, from whence the whole extension and magnificence of the central nave, the excellent paintings on the dome, and the immense proportions of the main altar may be commanded. One can also see for oneself that the statues of Saint Peter and Saint Paul, located in the upper part, enormous masses of bronze, are fashioned with delicate and exquisite ability, not including the innumerable architectural details which enhance the majestic construction **(pages 39-52-53).**

Starting from this corridor there are four staircases which lead us to the great tower of the dome whose circumference 82,70 metres, and whose first structure or drum has eight windows arranged in arches almost 10 metres high. Beneath the starting point of the dome an exterior cornice of great width, with a railing, runs like a circular balcony (four spiral staircases opened into the thickness of the pilars lead up to it) from which one can look out over the entire plan of the Monastery and of all the buildings which compose it, the gardens and orchards which surround it, the villages of the Seat and Villa de El Escorial, the Casitas for recreation, the woods, the Sierra and the vast plain in wide and beautiful perspective.

A further four exterior staircases rise to the lantern which surmounts the dome and which has eight square 5 metres windows. On top of the cupola above the lantern there rises a stone needle finishing with a bronze globe two meters in diameter. Halfway up the stone needle, a gilded plaque marks the spot where Philip II ordered various relics of Saint Peter, Saint Barbara and others to be placed. The two needles on the towers of the Kings' Court also have similar chests or boxes containing relics.

The Pantheons

The door leading to the Pantheon of the Kings is located in the passage from the church to the Sacristy.

It was Philip II's idea to build a crypt beneath the main altar for the royal pantheon, but he was unable to see the beginning of the works. His son, Philip III, wishing to comply with his father's will and thus complete the royal foundation, started the works in 1617 under the direction of the master architect Juan Gómez de Mora, but the plans were also committed to the architect and Roman nobleman Juan Bautista Crescensi, who conserved the circular form which the Pantheon had right from the beginning and only reduced the pavement by five feet (1,40 metres) so that it would be more proportionate and have greater architectonic beauty. For the actual construction he commissioned Pedro de Lizargárate, from Vizcaya,

Altar del Panteón de los Infantes
Autel du Panthéon des Infants
Altar in the Infante´s Pantheon

Wandaltar in der Prinzengruft
Altaré del Panteon degli Infanti
Altar do Panteão de Infantes

Araña en bronce dorado
Suspention en bronze doré
Chandelier of gilt bronze

Unter und Seitenansicht des Kronleuchters
Lampadario in bronzo dorato
Lustre em bronze dourado

Sepulcros de Infantas
Tombeaux d´Infantes
Sepulchres of Infantas

Infantengräber
Sepolcri delle Infanti
Sepulcros das Infantas

Panteón de Reyes
Panthéon des Rois
Pantheon of the King´s

Pantheon der Koenig
Panteon dei Re
Panteao dos Reis

Lavinia Fontana: Sagrada Familia con San Juanito
Lavinia Fontana: La Sainte Famille avec Saint Jean enfant
Lavinia Fontana: Holy Family with St. John

Lavinia Fontana: Die heilige Familie mit dem Johannesknaben
Lavinia Fontana: Sacra Famiglia con S. Giovanni Battista bamb
Lavinia Fontana: Sagrada Família com São Joãozinho

La adoración de la Sagrada Forma, por Claudio Coello
L´adoration de la Sainte Hostie, par Claudio Coello
Worshipping of the Host, by Claudio Coello

Die Verehrung der Sagrada Forma, von Claudio Coello
L´adorazione della Sacra Forma, di Claudio Coello
A Adoração da Sagrada Hóstia, por Claudio Coello

Altar del Santísimo Sacramento   Der Altar der Sakristei
Autel de Saint Sacrement   Altare del Santissimo Sacramento
Altar of the Holy Sacrament   Altar do Santíssimo Sacramento

and so industriously was the work carried out that in a little over two years marble covering had already been placed up to the starting point of the cupola, some of the urns and preparations were completed, and a great part of the bronze which was to decorate it was gilded. But in 1621 the King died and work was suspended for some 22 years. One may well understand the damage caused through the abandonment of the work for such a long time, and this was aggravated by the springing of a well in the crypt itself, which disunited and spoilt the marble slabs and turned it into a cistern. The difficulties were so great in number that everyone advised the king to build the Pantheon elsewhere in the Monastery, but the skill and knowledge of Fr. Nicolás from Madrid, a vicar at that time, found an answer to all the problems, expounding to the King the possibility and economy of certain works. Philip IV accepted his plan (drainage of the water, airing and illumination, and the construction of a staircase leading to it) and appointed him director and supervisor of the work. On November 1, 1645, work was renewed with the plans and designs for the staircase, the pavement, altar and door. Alonso Carbonell, His Majesty's architect, undertook the plans and designs, and they were executed by the marble-worker Bartolomé Zumbigo, who lived in Toledo. Nine years later, on March 16, 1654, Philip IV was able to inaugurate the Royal Pantheon.

After descending seven steps, a beautiful door, a fine combination of symmetry, with a two leaf grill door of gilded bronze and fashioned balustrades, leads into the Pantheons. Over the cornice at the end of the first structure, a slab of black Italian marble with gilded ornaments and bronze letters also gilded, contains a Latin inscription alluding to the construction of the Pantheon and which, when translated reads:

To Omnipotent and Almighty God. A Holy Place dedicated by the piety of the Austrias to the mortal remains of the Catholic Kings who await the promised day, beneath the high altar of the Restorer of Life. Charles V, the most illustrious of Emperors, desired this final resting place for himself and for those of his line; Philip II, the most prudent of Kings, selected it; Philip III, a truly pious Prince, commenced the work; Philip IV, great for his clemency, constancy and religion, enlarged, embellished and ended it in the year of Our Lord, 1654.

Above the inscription there is an arch-shaped frontispiece divided in the centre to accomodate the royal coat-of-arms. On either side of it there are two bronze figures made in Italy which depict Human Nature weakened (on the right) and Hope (on the left).

Of notable effect is the *staircase* which descends to the Pantheons, all constructed with precious marble from San Pablo de los Montes (Toledo) and with jasper from Tortosa "so well assembled and united that it appears to be a single piece". It consists of 34 steps and three landings: the first flight has 13 steps and two simulated doors, made from mahogany and ebony, however, they are purely ornamental; the second flight also consists of 13 steps and has a further two doors, the one on the right leading into the Sacristy of the Pantheon and the "pudrideros" (temporary vaults); the one on the left to the Pantheon of the Infantes and to further "pudrideros". On this landing, the direction of the staircase turns to the right, resulting in a change which brings great movement, "executed with skill and beauty". Descending another seven steps, a third landing marks the end of the staircase, and in it a grilled bronze door opens, similar to the one at the entrance which leads into the *Pantheon of the Kings.*

Pantheon of the Kings

It is built beneath the high altar of the Basilica. It is octagonal in shape, 10 metres in diameter and 10,60 in height; it is
entirely covered with precious marble and jasper from Tortosa
and Toledo, finely burnished and with all kinds of ornamentations and moundings of gilded bronze. The paving is made with
variously coloured marble and jasper shaped like a star in the
centre. A socle of half a meter circumscribes the hall and above
it at equal distances in all its periphery, there rise Corinthian pilasters made from jasper, with bronze bases and capitals,
which, at a height of 4,50 metres, supports a richly decorated
architrave, two metres in width, and from its cornice springs
the cupola which rises to 4,50 metres, forming 8 lunettes 1,70
metres high, covered with black marble from Vizcaya. Those on
the eastern side serve as windows which receive a third light
from the Patio de los Mascarones. On the opposite side there is
another which leads to the Pantheon of the Infantes and yet
another between these which leads to the royal chamber. **(p. 68-
69).**

Of the eight sides of the octagon, in elevation, two are
occupied, one by the altar and the other, opposite, by the door.
The other six contain the sepulchral urns of grey marble, 2
metres long, 0,84 high and 0,70 wide, of elegant Baroque design supported by four lion claws in gilded bronze. In the centre
of the urns in a bronze plate, one may read in black relief letters the name of the King or Queen whose remains it contains.
The urns, 26 in all, are grouped in black marble shelves, four in
each side and two over the door. The ones corresponding to the
Kings are on the left (Gospel), those of the Queen Mothers of
Crown Princes on the right (Epistle), except for Elizabeth of
Bourbon, first wife of Philip IV, buried here by express wish of
the Monarch. The bodies were arranged in chronological order.

The Kings who rest here are: Charles I of Spain and V of Germany, Emperor and King (1500-1556); Philip II (1527-1598); Philip III (1578-1621); Philip IV (1605-1665); Charles II (1661-1700); Louis I (1707-1724); Charles III (1716-1788); Charles IV (1748-1819); Ferdinand VII (1784-1833); Elizabeth II (1831-1904); Alfonso XII (1857-1885); and Francis of Assisi, King Consort as husband of Elizabeth II (1822-1902). The Queens are: Elizabeth, Empress, wife of Charles V (1503-1539); Anne, the fourth wife of Philip II (1549-1580); Margaret wife of Philip III (1584-1611); Elizabeth, first wife of Philip IV (1603-1644); Mary Anna second wife of Philip IV (1634-1696); Mary Louise, first wife of Philip V (1668-1714); Mary Amalia, wife of Charles III (1724-1760); Mary Louise, wife of Charles IV (1751-1819); Mary Christine, fourth wife of Ferdinand VII (1806-1878).

Those missing are: Philip V (1683-1746), who lies buried in the church at La Granja together with his second wife, Elizabeth of Farnesio; and Ferdinand VI (1713-1759), who lies buried in the Royal Salesas in Madrid, together with his wife, Barbara of Braganza.

The altar is fashioned with green marble from Genoa, with ornamentation and a gilded bronze frontal, depicting the *burial of Christ,* the work of Fr. Eugenio de la Cruz and Fr. Juan de la Concepción, lay brothers of the Monastery. Above the altar table two columns support an entablature, all made from the same green marble, finishing which reads "resurrection nostra". In the intercolumniation above the altar, there is a great bronze crucifix (1,40 metres high) by Domenico Guidi, with a black marble cross from Vizcaya. The splendid chandelier **(p. 66)** in gilded bronze, was also made in Genoa for this Pantheon by Virgilio Fanelli. It is octagonal in shape, 2 metres tall, with 24 arms, distributed in three levels and the axis, like

the rest of it, adorned with a multitude of volutes ("rocailles"), figures of small angels and little animals, the four
Evangelists, military trophies, and ending in a great royal crown
and rosette pendant. The gilded bronze angels which are placed
between every two pilasters and half-way up support candelabra, are the work of Clemente Censore from Milan.

The Royal Pantheon, extremely adorned, is a memorable
example of the Baroque art of the time.

Besides the artists already named, the sculptors Francesco
Generino, Giovanni Antonio Ceroni, Pietro Gatto, and the
bronze workers and founders, Giuliano Spagna, Giovanni
Battista Berinci and Francuccio Francucci, also worked for this
Pantheon.

Pantheon of the Infantes

In order to reach it, one must ascend the staircase to the
second landing, where it is divided, and then descend on the
right. On the entrance there is a slab of grey marble with a
Latin Inscription in gilded bronze letters which, when translated, reads:

*To Omnipotent and Almighty God, Elizabeth II, following
piously the steps of her predecessors, began to erect this tomb
with her accustomed splendour, which in honour of the relati-
ves and descendents of Kings is consecrated for the reception
of the remains of Queen Consorts who die without having borne
Princes, and of those of Princes and Infantes. Alphonso XII,
Prince of valiant spirit, for whom all Spain mourns, continued
religiously with the work but, surprised by death, was unable
to finish it. During the reign of Alphonso XIII, long may he live,
his most prudent mother, Mary Christine, the Regent, piously
continuing with the help of God, completes, perfected and finished it with all happiness in the year of Our Lord, 1886."*

Doña Elizabeth commissioned the project to the royal architect José Segundo de Lema (1862). Alphonso XII continued the work in 1877, but it was not finished until 1888, under the Regency of Mary Christine of Hapsbourg-Lorraine. There are 9 sepulchral chambers, five beneath the Sacristy, one beneath the Prior's Cell and three beneath the Capitular Chambers. The walls are covered with white marble from Florence and Carrara; the paving is of white and grey marble (Carrara and Bardiglio). Each of the chambers has a corresponding marble altar.

Ponciano Ponzano, a sculptor from Madrid, modelled the heralds, the sculptures and the ornaments which were fashioned in Carrara, from local marble by the Italian sculptor Jacobo Bartta di Leopoldo.

The most outstanding sepulchres in the *First Chapel,* are those which correspond to the Infanta Luisa Carlota de Borbón **(p. 67),** daughter of the King and Queen of the two Sicilies (1804-1844), with a kneeling life-size statue of the Infanta, in gilded bronze, the work of Ponzano and of the architect Domingo Gómez de la Puente who designed the sepulchre of white marble from Carrara; that of the *Dukes of Montpensier* (infanta Luisa Fernanda, sister of Elizabeth II (1832-1897) and her husband, Antonio of Orleans (1824-1890) and those of her two daughters Christine (1852-1879) and Amalia (1851-1870) each with a beautiful white Carrara marble statue, one of them signed by Aimé Millet of Paris, 1880. Finally we shall mention the altar painting *The Descent from the Cross,* by C. Cagliari; it has Valencia and Cabra marble borders and a moulding of porphyry. In the fourth chamber is the tomb of the Infanta Mary Teresa of Bourbon (sister of Alphonso XIII), designed by the architect Landecho; the material is dark marble and gilded bronze.

The tomb of don John of Austria, illegitimate son of Charles V, defeater of the Turks at Lepanto, is in the fifth chamber, right in the centre; upon it lies his statue, armed for war and with a sword between his hands. It was modelled by Ponzano an executed by the Italian sculptor Giuseppe Galleoti; the entire sepulchre is of Carrara marble (XIX Century).

In the sixth chamber is the childrens' mausoleum for the Infantes, or twenty-sided polygonal rotunda, in Carrara marble over dark marble socles, a work of little artistic merit. It contains 60 recesses. On the altar is the *Holy Family with Saint Juanito,* all watching the sleeping Child, a beautiful work by Lavinia Fontana, painted in 1590. **(P. 70)**.

Antesacristy

Ascending from the Pantheons one enters again the *Porch* of the *Sacristy,* or Antesacristy, a room 7 metres square, paved with white and grey marble. The walls, up to the cornice, are painted red ochre, and from thence begins the vault exquisitely painted by Nicolás Granello, in grotesque style. The eastern wall is taken up with a grey marble fountain with recesses on the upper part, and beneath each one there are fine little angel heads in gilded bronze, which are the spouts which pour water through their mouths into a great basin. It all ends in an architrave and cornice with pedestals and globes. At the sides of the fountain (4,50 metros long by 1 metre wide) there are two similar doors, one of which leads to the Pantheons. A further three large doors open into this room, one leading to the Sacristy, another to the church, and on the western side another which leads to the main cloister.

The walls of this Chamber are decorated with thirteen paintings of the indulgence conceded to El Escorial.

It is not necessary to pass directly into the Antesacristy but from the Basilica you may leave again by the porch and enter on your left into the old, main Convent porter's lodge, a small, vaulted room called the *"Sala de Secretos" (Secrets Room)* because of its special acoustic conditions which allow visitors to "tell secrets" in a whisper from its corners. From thence, one may enter the *Sala de la Trinidad,* so called because of the vast canvas dealing with this subject, the work of José de Ribera, which was hung there. Today it is adorned with a red velvet cloth and a large shield bearing the arms of Philip II. Besides these there are various pictures, three large paintings of battles, of which two depict the *Battle of Lepanto:* the massed Armada leaving the port of Messina under the command of don John of Austria and the Christian and Turkish ships in line of battle, both painted by Lucas Cambiasso, Luchetto; the third depicts the *battle of the Dunes or of Newport,* and is of the Flemish school. The sketch of the *martyrdom, or beheading of Santiago* (in the Capitular Halls) is by Navarrete, el Mudo; the *Virgin suckling the Child* is copied from the Parmesan by Luis de Carvajal; the *Holy Family with St. Ann and St. John* is from the Italian school, and a *Philosopher.*

Sacristy

Among the group of paintings exhibited in the Sacristy and in the Capitular Halls, some may be classified as in their original order although there are many others which have left to form the new Pinacotheca, where, adequately installed, they may be admired and studied in greater comfort and in all the splendour of their outstanding quality.

La adoración de la Sagrada Forma, por Claudio Coello
L´adoration de la Sainte Hostie, par Claudio Coello
Worshipping of the Host, by Claudio Coello

Die Verehrung der Sagrada Forma, von Claudio Coello
L´adorazione della Sacra Forma, di Claudio Coello
A adoração da Sagrada Hóstia, por Claudio Coello

Sacristía: Vista general
La Sacristie: Vue générale
Sacristy: General view

Sakristei: Ansicht
Sagrestia: Vista generale
Sacristia: Vista geral

Ribera: La adoración de los pastores
Ribera: L´adoration des pasteurs
Ribera: The adoration of the shepherds

Ribera: Die Anbetung der Hirten
Ribera: L´adorazione dei pastori
Ribera: A Adoração dos pastores

84

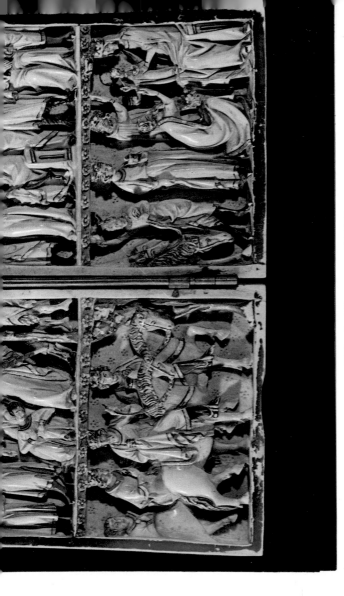

Díptico de marfil
Diptycue en ivoire
Ivory dipthyc

Diptychon
Dittico di avorio
Díptico de marfim

Sala Capitular (derecha)
Salle Capitulaire (de droite)
Capitular Hall (right)

Kapitelsaal (rechts)
Sala Capitolare (destra)
Sala Capitular (direita)

Sala Capitular (izquierda)
Salle Capitulaire (de gauche)
Capitular Hall (left)

Kapitelsaal (rechts)
Sala Capitolare (sinistra)
Sala Capitular (esquerda)

Casulla "La vida de Cristo"
Chasuble "La vie de Christ"
Chasuble "Christ's Life"

Ornat mit Bildstickerei
Pianeta di prete "La vita di Cristo"
Casula "A vida de Cristo"

The great vaulted chamber of the Sacristy (30 by 9 metres and nearly 11 metres high) occupies part of the Eastern passage of the lower cloister in the Patio of the Evangelists; it receives light from it through five windows at ground level and through a further nine small ones high up over the cornice, to which correspond nine recesses containing as many windows in the opposite wall. Between the large windows there alternate four cupboards made of rich woods, where sacred vessels and articles of worship are kept; also in the opposite wall (western) and along the entire length of it, runs the precious chest of drawers made from fine woods, inlaid and decorated with mosaics (acana, mahogany, ebony, terebinth, cedar, walnut and boxwood). It consists of two parts, the lower one has just been described, and is divided by pilasters into seven equal parts, each one containing four drawers, finishing in a large walnut table; the second part, Corinthian in style, rests upon this table, with its columns, architrave, frieze and cornice exquisitely carved; the intercolumniation panels are the doors for further cupboards or closets where vessels and sacred ornaments are kept. In the centre hangs a beautiful Baroque mirror, its frame made of silver and its adornments of rock crystal, a present from the Queen doña María Ana of Austria, the mother of Charles II, and on either side of it there are a further six smaller ones conveniently spaced out, with silver-plated frames, finely fashioned by the Hieronymite lay-brother Fr. Eugenio de la Cruz. The vaulted ceiling is painted with grotesques, representing great sechiars with various ornaments between the projecting ribs, the work of Nicolás Granello and Fabricio Castello. The paving is of white and grey marble (p. 72).

The collection of paintings exhibited in it come in the following order: beginning on the righthand side (Epistle); the *Drunken Noah with his Sons* (Cam mocks his father whilst

Shem and Japheth cover up his nakedness with a mantle);
the Prayer in the Garden; The false prophet, Baal, (riding a
female donkey beats it mercilessly; the animal speaks to him,
recriminating him for this, just as an angel passes by with
a sword), the three works by Lucas Giordano, called Jordán
de España (1632-1705), *Christ crucified,* by Titian; *Saint Job,*
by Lucas Jordán; *Saint Peter in prison* (Freeing of St. Peter
by the angel when he had been put in prison), with most
beautiful contrasts of light and shade by José de Ribera
(1588-1656); *The heroine Jael and Sisara* (Jael is in an attitude of prayer to the divine auxiliary before hammering a
nail through the temples of Sisara, Chief of the Canaanites,
his enemies, who lies drunken at his feet), again painted by
Jordán. On the left hand side, the *Transfiguration,* a copy from
Raphael; *The Virgin with Child and little St. John,* from the
Italian School; *Saint Peter,* deep in contemplation, a bust in
imitation of Lucas Jordán; *The Virgin, the Child Jesus and
St. Ann, who offers some fruit to Him,* by Miguel Coxcie (1497-
1592); *the Martyrdom of St. Agnes* (the Saint in the middle
of a blazing fire seems to pray and the flames pursue her
torturers), by Juan Gómez; the *Holy Family with a vision of
the martyrdom of Jesus* (the Virgin, St. Joseph and the Child,
standing, stretches out His little arms to some angels who
bear a cross and the other articles connected with His Passion;
high above, the Eternal Father), by José Simonelli; *Ecstasy of
St. John of God,* by L. Jordán; St. *John the Baptist,* by Sebastián Herrera Barnuevo; *St. Anthony,* from the 17th Century
Spanish School, *Saint Paul; The Holy Family,* from the Flemish school; *St. Peter.*

The most outstanding picture in the Sacristy is the one
which covers the altar, depicting the *Sacred Form,* the work
of Claudio Coello, the last great figure of the Madrilenian

School, who, in this picture achieved his masterpiece **(pages 71-72-81).** It represents the religious celebration which was held on October 19, 1680, for the solemn transfer of the Sacred Form from another part of the Monastery to its new Chapel in the Sacristy, in the presence of the King and the nobles in his court. It is all admirably composed in a most profound perspective (of the Sacristy itself) "so realistic, so correctly drawn, with so much strength of colour, with such power of reproduction in the perspective, that everything depicted in the painting seems to move, and come out of it."

An infinite number of people are pictured in the canvas, with exceptional mastery: the King, Charles II, kneeling, worshipping the *Sacred Form* which is carried by Fr. Francisco de los Santos, Prior of the Monastery; behind the King are seen Father Marcos de Herrera and the nobles of the Court, the Dukes of Medinaceli and Pastrana, the Count of Baños, the Marquis de la Puebla, and the first son of the Duke of Alba; and, on the second plane, the religious Community of the Hieronymites singing; the painter's portrait is the first of the personages on the left, without a wig and with side whiskers **(p. 71-81).** Higher up in the painting, there are various figures which represent some virtues and small angels gathering a curtain.

To get a better comprehension of the painting, the history of the Sacred Form and of the miracle which made it so famous must be remembered. During the religious wars which desolated the Low Countries, the Zwinglian heretics entered the Dutch city of Garcum desecrating its temples, and in the Cathedral they even trampled underfoot the consecrated Forms. In the one which is preserved in El Escorial they tore three holes which seem to have been produced by the nails of the shoes of whoever stepped upon it, and from these holes blood started to pour, the stains from which still exist. One of the heretics, frightened and marvelling at the miracle, told of it to Dean John Vander Delph, who took the Sacred Form, both of them fleeing to Malinas, at that time an imperial city, and depositing it in the Convent of Saint Francis, where it acquired extraordinary fame from whence, so as to avoid further mishaps, it was taken to Vienna and then to Prague. Later, it so happened that the precious relic should be presented to Philip II, in 1592, by Rudolph II, Emperor of Germany and King of Hungary. The piety of Philip II caused so priceless a present to be deposited along with the infinite amount of relics that he had been collecting in the Basilica of El Escorial. Charles II became particularly devoted to the Sacred Form when he learned its history and it was his wish to have it stand out in a special Chapel.

As for the construction of the Chapel, retable and the altar themselves, it should be remembered that don Fernando de Valenzuela, the king's favourite, who fell into disgrace in 1677, and pursued by order of don John Joseph of Austria, he took refuge in the Monastery with the King's consent. The Duke of Medinasidonia and other nobles besieged El Escorial, finally entering in a disorderly manner, profaning the sanctity of the place, desecrating relics and infuriating the monks. They were excomunicated by the Prior Fr. Marcos de Herrera and. in order to lift the punishement, the Pope imposed the penance of erecting a new and sumptuous chapel. The humbled Charles II, frightened by the sanction, promised to fulfil the penance and the Chapel was inaugurated in 1684.

The *altar* and *retable* in the Sacristy occupy the south wall and constitute the centre of the total decoration in the place which, in its lower part, represents a true Corinthian facade, although the cornices are still highly ornate in outline, according to the Baroque style of the time. The material used was jasper and marble inlaid and richly combined, with an abundance of gilded bronze for the decorative complementary articles (bases, capitals, shields, foliage, medallions). The design and work is by José del Olmo, architect to Charles II, and the bronze ornamental work was carried out by the Italian Francisco Filippini, watchmaker and bronze worker of the Royal Palace **(p. 82)**.

The lower part is composed of a high pedestal above which rise two central pilasters whose shafts are decorated with precious bronze. Next to the pilasters there are two extensive columns of 2,80 metres. A further two equal columns on the extreme right and left form three hollow spaces, the intercolumn in the centre flanking the altar which cuts the pedestal, and in its opening there is a transparent chapel, 2,50 metres wide by 5,60 high, which breaks the cornice in the first part and reaches the height of the second. Between the side intercolumniations there are similar doors made of fine woods with tortoise shell and bronze decorations, with the shields of Castile and León, and above the lintel there is also a lion with a sceptre and globe held aloft in its claws, all made of gilded bronze. Over the lintel on top of each door a recess is formed, finished with a pointed arch with white marble reliefs which depict respectively the handing over of the Sacred Form to Rudolph II of Germany and to Philip II. Over the keystone of these recesses there are two eagles fully extended with the collar of Toison in their beaks, also fashioned from gilded bronze. Finally, the whole of this first part ends with a cornice which is broken up by the retable.

The second part, above it, forms the crowning of the altar in the centre, framed by two short marble buttresses above which the figures are grouped, and which support the broken frontispiece and rocailles. Bronze foliage, seraphims in whi-

te marble from Genoa in the capitals and, closing the frontispiece, bearing a large plaque with an allusive inscription, two
bronze angels sitting over the volutes of the frontispiece form a
sumptuous crowning, rich and profuse, and well in keeping
with the taste of the time. On its sides, over the doors, this
second part is composed of white marble medallions with reliefs which depict the abuses caused by the heretics to the Sacred Form (which is honoured without corruption on the altar
of the Sacristy) and the entering in the Franciscan Order of one
of these heretics who was converted by the miracle. There
remain two medallions flanked between the figures of two children in white marble with bronze torch holders and all this is
finished with a seraphim who bears aloft a large royal crown.
The entire altar ends following the curve of the dome.

The frontal and altar steps over which this rises are made
from brightly gilded copper and hammer designs with figures
and stories of the saints, Flemish work from the Sixteenth Century and completed by Lesmes del Moral.

The altar is completely covered by the painting of C. Coello
which serves as a veil or transparency to the Blessed Sacrament **(p. 71-72)** and which is drawn back only twice a
year: on Jubilee days, the feast day of St. Michael (29th September) and of St. Simon and St. Jude (28th October). The
picture is lowered by means of a winch and is kept beneath the
paving. When this is done, a magnificent crucifix can be seen,
with the figure of Christ beautifully modelled and shaped in
gilded bronze, the work of Pedro Tacca **(p. 72),** and also a
large shrine, also gilded, in Gothic-Roman style (Cathedral style) 1,60 metres high, designed by the Royal painter don Vicente
López, begun in 1829 by Ignacio Millán and finished in 1834
in Madrid by Francisco Pecul. It contains various relics and is
decorated with 40 statuettes and 10 busts. The rich holy vessel

of Elizabeth II, presented by her in 1852, a work fashioned in Madrid by Carlos Pizzala, of excellent silversmith work and clustered with stones, is one of the gems wich disappeared in 1936.

The Sacristy's "camerin" behind the retable, covered in marble and decorated in bronze, is the work of Francisco Ricci, José del Olmo and Francisco Filippi.

The Capitulary Halls

The Capitulary Halls occupy almost the whole of the south passage of the low cloister. They earned their name because they were used by the Hieronymites for their Capitular meetings. Today they form a Museum of valuable paintings, sacred garments, and articles of a singular richness and art (silverwork, ivory). The whole group consists of four spacious consecutive halls: one in the centre, almost square (9 by 8 metres) where the entrance door is to be found, and which may be considered as the vestibule and two large chambers on the right and the left (22 by 8 metres) called respectively the Sala Vicarial and the Sala Prioral, and adjoining the latter there is a further, smaller room known as the lower Prior's cell. They all receive light through windows on the south side which correspond equally to those of the Sacristy, windows rising from the floor, and further, smaller ones higher up over them which correspond to recesses or blind windows in the opposite wall, windows which supply the necessary light and clarity to admire all that is exhibited in these halls.

All the halls have vaulted ceilings painted beautifully with frescoes in Renaissance grotesque style, with biblical figures and Saints, the work of Granello and Fabricio, the sons of Bergamasco (Capitular Halls) and of Francisco de Urbino (low Priorial cell), with fine decorative effect. The style is similar to that used to decorate the vaulted roof of the Sacristy, but with an infinite variety of decorative elements (allegories, natural fauna, mythology, fantasy, foliage, rosettes) which fill up the compartments and the large girders which outline the arches. In the centre of the vaulted roof of the vestibule, in Pompeian style, is represented a sky with its clouds through which angels descend with a crown of laurel, and in the recesses hollowed out over the doors and windows can be seen *Job wounded* and *the Prophets.* The two large halls produce a most beautiful effect by the distribution of their paintings, as in girded arches which divide up the vaulted roofs with horizontal bands and give them a singular perspective **(p. 86-87).**

Hanging from the walls there are the following paintings: *Portrait of Innocence X,* a copy from Velázquez by Pietro Martire Neri; two *large flower pots* and two small ones by Daniel Seghers (1590-1661) and the *Adoration of the Shepherds* and *the Adoration of the Kings,* in Veronese style. In one of the frontispieces is exhibited an *altar frontal* embroidered in great relief by D. Alphonso XIII in 1910, who came from Las Leandras of Seville.

In the centre of the vestibule, an *angel* somewhat larger than normal, upon a pedestal, supports a lectern which was used as a chorister's desk; it is fashioned from gilded bronze and was made in Amberes by the Flemish Juan Simón in 1571.

Altar portátil del Emperador Carlos V
L'autel portatif de l'Empereur Charles V
Portable altar of the Emperor Charles V

Reisealtar Kaiser Karls V
Altare portatile dell'Imperatore Carlo V
Altar portátil do Imperador Carlos V

97

Capa "La vida de Cristo"　　　Pluviale mit Bildstickerei
Chape "La vie de Christ"　　　Piviale "La vita di Cristo"
Cope "Christ's Life"　　　　　Capa "A vida de Cristo"

Breviario del Emperador Carlos V
Missel de l'Empereur Charles V
Breviary of the Emperor Charles V

Brevier Kaiser Karls V
Breviario dell'Imperatore Carlo V
Breviário do Imperador Carlos V

Vista general de la Biblioteca
Vue générale de la Bibliothèque
General view of the Library

Ansicht in die Bibliotheke
Vista generale della Biblioteca
Vista geral da Biblioteca

El dios Pan   Der Gott Pan
Le dieu Pan   Il dio Pan
The god Pan   O deus Pan

Escalera principal del Monasterio
Le Grand Escalier du Monastère
Main staircase of the Monastery

Das Treppenhaus
Scalone principale del. Monastero
Escada Principal do Mosteiro

Detalle de la bóveda, pintada por Lucas Jordán
Détail de la voûte, peinte par Lucas Jordán
Detail of the vault, painted by Lucas Jordán

Wand, bemahll von Lucas Jordán
Particolare della volta, dipinta da Lucas Jordán
Pormenor da abóbada, pintada por Lucas Jordán

The right hand Capitular Hall (Sala Vicarial)

As one enters, and over the pointed arches of both fore-parts, there are some classical framings with broken frontispie-ce, harbouring two medallions or reliefs of porphyry on a back ground of white marble and gilded frames representing the *Head of the Saviour*. Similarly, in the left hand Capitular Hall (Sala Prioral), there is represented the *Virgin with the Child*. They are both illustrated with Latin inscriptions attributed to the humanist Benito Arias Montano **(p. 86)**.

The paintings in this Hall come in the following order: on the right hand side, *St. John the Baptist and St. John the Evangelist* (standing in a field) an anonymous work from the Sixteenth Century Spanish School; five great works by Juan Fernández de Navarrete, el Mudo (1526-1579), the most notable among the group of Spanish painters who penetrated into El Escorial; *St. Hieronymo in penitence, the Flagellation of the Lord* (bound to the column in a courtyard, two executioners begin to flog Him; the *martyrdom of Santiago Apostol,* the best painting by El Mudo, signed in 1571 (the Saint is kneeling and dying be-cause of the wound which his executioner has dealt him in the neck; in the background is represented on a plain the battle of Clavijo); the *Holy Family with Saint Joaquim and Saint Ann;* as a picturesque detail one can see in the foreground a dog and a cat quarrelling and a partridge on the other side; and *the Lord's birth* (the Virgin and St. Joseph, kneeling, worhsip the newly born child who stands out in a bright splendour) by F. Zúccaro; and the *Adoration of the Shepherds*. In the lower fore-part is exhibited an altar table on which has been installed the so-called *portable altar of the Emperor,* for it is supposed to be the one which Charles V carried with him into battle. It is made from bronze and silver with enamel and takes the form of a retable, crowned by the frontispiece and separated into five horizontal zones in which alternate reliefs and statuettes divided up by little columns (atlantispilasters in the lower part), of the four classical styles (Doric, Ionic, Corinthian and Composed) in the four upper ones, forming a most beautiful ensemble **(p. 97).** At the sides are two chandelier-vessels of gilded and engraved bronze. Hanging on the right and the left are two small stained glass windows which contain, respectivelvy, a white marble relief which depicts *St. Hieronymo penitent* by Fray Eugenio de Torices, and which is framed by a wooden chapel and a silver *Calvary* in repoussé work with an ebony frame. The left hand wall is again adorned with paintings: *St. Peter; the Assumption* and *St. Augustin in an attitude of writing,* both by Bartolomé Vicente; *Christ Crucified; St. Hieronymo* (head and shoulders) by Matías Torres (?); *Dolorosa,* a copy of the Italian School; and the *Holy Family with little St. John,* also of the Italian School.

The left hand Capitular hall (Sala Prioral)

Its forepart is decorated as has already been described, and the remainder is covered with paintings as follows:

Four pictures with *floral crowns* which contain a relief in greyish style with the following subjects: *Moses receiving the tablets of the Ten Commandments on Mt. Sinai; Cain and Abel; Jacob's dream* and *The sacrifice of Isaac,* all four by Mario de Fiori (1603-1673); the *Immaculate Virgin* by Vicente Carducho; the *Transfiguration,* a copy of Raphael; the *Praying Nazarite,* Italian School; the *Magdalene in Prayer,* a copy of Titian, by Lucas Jordán; *St. Bartholomew,* anonymous; *Dolorosa* (half-length), a copy of Titian; *Noah after the flood* (surrounded by his family he builds an altar to offer sacrifices to God), by André Vaccaro; *Adoration of the Shepherds,* by Ribera; another *Adoration of the Shepherds* by Pablo Matteis (1662-1728), with only head and shoulder studies of the figures; the *Most Holy Trinity* by Ribera; *The Doubt of Saint Thomas* (figures with head and shoulders only), by Matteis; *Adoration of the Shepherds* by Ribera **(p. 83);** and the *Annunciation of Mary,* by Francisco Rizzi (1608-1685).

The lower Prior's cell

The vaulted roof of this hall, the work of Francisco de Urbino, represents the *Judgement of Solomon.*

Standing out from the artistic objects which are exhibited in the lower Prior's cell are the rich *liturgical vestments* of the Sixteenth Century, richly embroidered in silk and gold in the Monastery itself, after the school of the "extremeño" of Guadalupe (7 show cases) although its first master was Fray Lorenzo de Montserrat, so named because he came from that monastery in Cataluña. The four articles exhibited are extremely rich and brilliant; the socalled *Terno (vestment) in green,* in silk damask of this colour embroidered with gold and silver on green velvet with shields bearing the emblems of the Passion and the Gridiron of the Monastery; *the Terno of the office of the dead or of the skulls,* in black and silver velvet brocade ringed with embroidery of the Renaissance style, with an abundance of spangles also of silver and funeral emblems, of skulls and flutes; *the Terno of the feast of St. Lorenzo,* of brocade and red ringed velvet, so called because among its

embroidery stand out the palms and the gridirons connected
with the martyrdom of the Saint; finally the *Terno of the Life
of Christ,* in white brocade ringed with gold and embroidered
with fringes and brushes with almost the pictorial technique of
"shaded gold" with scenes depicting passages from the Life
of the Redeemer. It is a most beautiful exemplary **(pages
88-98).**

In another show case is the ivory collection; the small
rectangular *chest of relics,* made of bone roughly engraved
with the Pantocrator and the Tetramorfos and various scenes
from the Sacred History; Castilian art from the Tenth or early
Eleventh Century; a small Gothic diptych, from those called
«the roses» because of the roses which decorate them, from
a Fourteenth Century Parisian workshop **(p. 84-5),** exquisitely worked, with scenes from the life of Jesus Christ; and
a group which depicts the Descent with delicate workmanship
from the Buen Retiro workshops of the Eighteenth Century.
From among the metalwork, gold and silverwork objects there
stands out a small *chest of relics of enamel from Thirteenth
Century Limoges,* rectangular, with a lid of two sloping sides,
which depicts on one of its larger sides the scene of the death
and burial of St. Thomas Becket. The plate on which the
pyx is carried is engraved in silver and coated in gold, in pla-
teresque, with the print of the artist Becerril, in Cuenca
(Sixteenth Century)' There is also a silver tray, supposedly
from the Sixteenth Century; a *shrine* in the form of a book, a
present from the Archbishop of Treveris to Philip II in 1571,
with five medallions inside, beautifully engraved in gilt silver;
two silver crowns of the Virgin of the Patronage, a chest or
gilt pix Spanish art from the Seventeenth Century with a
set of several filigree *wine vessels* from the time of Charles II; and various other objects in gilt bronze such as a *holy*

water basin with its water sprinkler. There are also various other pieces less precious but of great interest and rarity, as, for example; an *episcopal mitre* of dark purple silk, with various scenes from the Life of Christ and of the Virgin, with Apostles, Prophets and Patriarchs fashioned in mosaics with exquisite coloured feathers and with metallic brilliance, combined skillfully, a typical example of Mexican work of the Aztec Indians (Sixteenth Century), called feathered work, carried out under the direction of Spanish missionaries, following designs of artists who were also Spanish; a book containing drawings or designs which served as models to embroider the priestly robes and holy ornaments of the Monastery; and two paintings on octagonal agates which depict the *Descent from the Cross* and *St. Anthony of Padua,* attributed to Aníbal Caracci (1560-1609).

In the spaces which the cabinets leave free, an altar frontal made of porphyry overlaid with gilt silver, the work of the Hieronymite lay brothers, Fr. Eugenio de la Cruz and Fr. Juan de la Concepción (Seventeenth Century) and an alabaster templet of a kind similar to that in the Monstrance of the High Altar may be admired.

Main lower cloister

From the Capitular Halls which occupy the south side of the *main lower cloister,* access is gained to the cloister **(p. 113)** which is formed by a spacious granite gallery 56 metres long, by nearly 7 wide and 8 high with a cannon vaulted ceiling with lunettes, whose walls were decorated with great frescoes (the Life of Jesus Christ) by Peregrín Tibaldi (eastern side) which are the best, and by his disciples. The order of the subject matter for these frescoes begins on the North wall, in a door which is found there called the Door of Processions, since on all solemn occasions, processions enter and leave through this door. The first painting is the *Conception of the Virgin* announced by the angel to St. Joachim and St. Ann who are embracing in front of the Golden Door of Solomon's Temple; this story finishes on the opposite side of this same cloister door in which appears *The Last Judgement.* Following, we enumerate all the paintings, including those of the Stations: *Conception of the Virgin* or *Embrace of St. Joachim and St. Ann; The Birth of the Virgin; Presentation in the Temple; Betrothal of Mary and Joseph; The Annunciation; Visit of Our Lady to her cousin St. Elizabeth; Birth of Christ and Adoration of the Shepherds; Adoration of the Kings; The Purification of Our Lady; The Flight into Egypt; Slaughter of the Innocents: The Return from Egypt; Jesus tempted by Satan; The Choosing of the Apostles; The Resurrection of Lazarus; Jesus casting the Money-lenders out of the Temple; The Transfiguration of the Lord; The Last Supper; The Prayer in the Garden; The Arrest of Jesus in the Mount of Olives; Jesus in the house of Annas; Jesus in the house of Caiphas; Herod mocks Christ; The Scourging of Jesus; The Crowning with Thorns; Ecce Homo; Pilate washes his hands after condemning Jesus; Jesus on the road to Calvary; The Crucifixion; The Resurrection of the Lord; Jesus appears to the Virgin; The Marys near the Sepulchre; St. Peter and St. John in the Sepulchre of Jesus; Jesus appears as a Gardener to Mary Magdalene; Jesus appears to the Marys; Jesus appears to His disciples on the road to Emmaus; Appearance of Jesus in the Cenacle; Showing the wounds to St. Thomas; Appearance of Jesus to the Apostles fishing in the Sea of Tiberias; Ascension of the Lord; Ascension of Mary to the Heavens; Coronation of the Virgin;* and the *Last Judgement.*

The archways on the exterior of the cloister are closed with walnut and pine windows, painted on the outside. The pointed arches are closed with glass. The paving is of white and gray marble.

Two chapels or *stations* are formed in the angles, one on each wall, with a great retable and doors shaped like a diptych, painted inside and outside, the work of: Luis de Carvajal, *Adoration of the Shepherds* and *Adoration of the Kings* (north-eastern angle); Rómulo Cincinato, *Transfiguration* and *Last Supper* (south-western angle); Peregrín Tibaldi, *Calvary* and *Ressurection* (south-eastern angle); and Miguel Barroso, the *Coming of the Holy Spirit* and *Ascension of Christ* (north-western angle).

Main Staircase

In the centre of the western gallery, three arches open into the great staircase which used to be the main one and which connects the lower floor whith the great high cloister or Procession cloister **(p. 103)**. It was designed by Juan Bautista Castello, the Bergamasco "and because of its greatness, majesty and ornamentation it may be considered as one of the most notable pieces in the Monastery". It is 23 metres high, 8 wide and is formed from 52 one-piece granite steps, 4,40 metres in length; it begins with a single shaft to divide it in two in the wide landing half way up.

Its fresco decorations are notable; the well of the staircase contains 14 arches at top floor level; five of these are closed and contain painted panels which continue the subject matters of the Life of Jesus Christ from the cloister below; two are by Luchetto: *St. Peter and St. John next to the Lord's Sepulchre* and the *Appearance of Jesus to the Apostles in the Cenacle;*

three are by Tibaldi: *Appearance of the Lord to the Magdalene,
Appearance to the Holy Women* and *Appearance to the
disciples at Emmaus;* but the most outstanding work belongs
to Lucas Jordán who, in the time of Charles II, painted the
great frieze and the immense dome with extraordinary beauty
and insuperable style in the unbelievable time of seven months.
On the frieze he represented the battle, siege and surrender of
St. Quintín (on the south, west and northern sides) and the
foundation of the Monastery of San Lorenzo El Real de El Escorial (eastern side). "On three sides of the wide frieze located
between the two cornices, he represented, on the southern
side, the battle which precedded the assault on San
Quintín in which the French army was broken and the Constable Montmorency, along with his son, was taken prisoner with
several other French noblemen. In the western one he represented the distribution of the place, location of the batteries
and assault on the town; and in the northern one the moment
when the victorious soldiers presented to Manuel Filiberto,
Duke of Savoy, the banners taken in the assault and the prisoner, the Admiral of France, who defended it, and who can be
seen on horseback but with head bared and unarmed before
the Duke. On the eastern side Philip II can be seen on foot and
before him are the famous architects Juan Bautista de Toledo
and Juan de Herrera, accompanied by the eminent laybrother
Fr. Antonio de Villacastín, showing him the design and lay-out
of El Escorial. On the other end of this same canvas can be
seen part of the construction in its early stages and various
workers laying the foundations, carrying stones and other
workers placing them."

The cornice which runs over this frieze is perfectly gilded
as are the window frames. On each side of the latter there are
angels·leaning on shields engraved with the coat-of-arms of

Galería del claustro bajo
Galerie basse du cloître
Gallery of the Lower Cloister

Im unteren Hauptkreuzgang
Galleria del cniostro basso
Galeria do Claustro Baixo

Comedor de gala. Tapices de Bayeu y Castillo
Salle à manger d'apparat. Tapis de Bayeu et Castillo
Banquet Hall. Bayeu and Castillo Tapestries

Der Speisesaal. Wandteppiche von Bayeu und Castillo
Sala da pranzo di gala. Arazzi di Bayeu e Castillo
Sala de Jantar de gala. Tapetes de Bayeu e Castillo

114

Antesala de Embajadores. Tapices de Goya
Antichambre des Ambassadeurs. Tapis de Goya
Ambassador´s Lobby. Goya´s Tapestries

Das Vorzimmer des Gesandtensaals. Wandteppiche von Goya
Antisala degli Ambasciatori. Arazzi di Goya
Ante-sala de Embaixadores. Tapetes de Goya

Federico Zuccaro: La Anunciación de Nuestra Señora
Federico Zuccaro: L'Annonciation de la Vierge
Federico Zuccaro: Annunciation of Our Lady

Federico Zuccaro: Die Verkündigung
Federico Zuccaro: L'Annunciazione di Nostra Signora
Federico Zuccaro: A Anunciação de Nossa Senhora

Salón de Embajadores
Salon des Ambassadeurs
Ambassadors Hall

Der Gesandtensaal
Salone degli Ambasciatori
Salão de Embaixadores

Bayeu: Tapiz: El juego de boches
Bayeu: Tapis: Le jeu de boules
Bayeu: Tapestry: Playing ninepins

Bayeu: Wandteppich: Das Bocciaspiel
Bayeu: Arazzo: Il gioco della bocce
Bayeu: Tapête: O Jogo da laranjinha

119

Bayeu: Tapiz: El juego de la vaquilla
Bayeu: Tapis: Le jeu de la vachette
Bayeu: Tapestry: Children playing bullfigting

Bayeu: Wandteppich: Das Stierkampfspiel
Bayeu: Arazzo: Il gioco "della vaccherella"
Bayeu: Tapête: O Jogo da Vaquinha

Spain; and in their lunettes are medallions in imitation of porphyry, representing some of the victories of the Emperor
Charles V, except in the centre of the Eastern part where there
is a fake bronze engraving of the portrait of Philip IV, corresponding to that of Charles II on the western side.

On the vaulted ceiling, Jordán painted *the Glory* **(p. 104)**
in a grandiose style; high above is the throne of the Most Holy
Trinity surrounded by clouds, light and angels; on its right is the
Virgin with angels who are carrying the emblems of the Passion; opposite them are the Holy Kings, the Spaniards St. Her-
menegildo and St. Ferdinand, St. Henry (Emperor of Germany),
St. Eusebio (King of Hungary), St. Casimiro (Prince of Poland);
beneath, St. Hieronymous dressed as a Cardinal introducing
Charles V and Philip II, the former offering two crowns, those of
the Emperor and King of Germany and Spain, and the latter a
globe, a symbol of his power in the whole world. San Lorenzo,
too, approaches as mediator. In the four angles are the Cardinal Virtues and the groups from which they are derived; two
beautiful matrons symbolizing the Royal Majesty (southern side)
and the Catholic Church (north side), which give each other mu-
tual aid; to the west is pictured a balustrade upon which Charles II is leaning and explaining to his wife, Doña María Ana of
Neuburg and to his mother Doña Mariana of Austria, the sig-
nificance of this painting which he has commissioned.

Court of the Evangelists

The lower cloister encloses the Court of the Evangelists
(46,50 metres on each side), one of the most beautiful in the
world and one of the most exquisite creations of Juan de Herrera, a masterpiece of elegance and harmony **(p. 35)**. The
façades are composed of 12 arches on each side, forming two

series of arches, upper and lower, in Doric and Ionic style respectively; the upper series is finished with a balustrade. In the centre of the court rises an octagonal shrine, Doric in style, with an entablature similarly finished with a beautiful balustrade; a graceful cupola crowns the monument. The exterior is made of granite, harmonizing with the rest of the court, but its interior is covered with marble and jasper of different colours. On the larger sides of the octagon there open as many arches or portals; and on its lesser sides there are equal recesses containing 2 metre statues of the Evangelists: St. Matthew, St. Mark, St. Luke and St. John (who give the court its name) and their emblems: the angel, the lion, the bull and the eagle, the work of Juan Bautista Monegro in white Genoa marble. Each of the Evangelists has an open book in his hand, and written inside is a text from the respective Gospel in the language in which it was originally written: St. Matthew in Hebrew; St. Mark in Latin; St. Luke in Greek; and St. John in Syrian. Four small pools flank the shrine and the rest is beautiful garden with trimmed box-trees.

From the Court of the Evangelists may be seen one of the most beautiful architectural ensembles of the Monastery: the Cloister, specially the Dome, which display the ingenious mastery of Herrera and his classical concept of the Renaissance in its purest forms.

Entering the cloister once more and walking around it one comes across six doors: one in the middle of the north side (the Processional door); one on the south (to the Capitular Halls); two in the east (to the Sacristy); and two on the west, wide open, one corresponding to the so called *Old Church* and the other to the Porter's Lodge. One must go through the latter to reach the King's Court once more and the porch where the entrance and staircases may be found, leading to the high Cloister where the Library door opens.

The Library

The Library is another of the great riches which the Monastery of San Lorenzo de El Escorial contains. When Philip II created and installed it he exceeded his munificence in mounting it, in its content and endowment for its upkeep. His own books (4.000), those which he had brought from various places (Royal Chapel at Granada), the collections of erudites bought and acquired by special privileges, soon made the Library of El Escorial the most famous in Europe **(p. 100-101)**. Besides the king's own books, about 4.000 including printed volumes and manuscripts, delivered as the first lot in 1565, one must mention those of the Ambassador to Italy, don Diego Hurtado de Mendoza, a splendid collection above all of Italian books, manuscripts and rare incunabula, framed in the owner's colours (red and black, one on each cover, with gold vertical stripes and with gilded medallions in relief). 133 volumes were brought from the Royal Chapel in Granada, many of them coming from the Camara Regia of the Kings of Castile themselves (books of Alphonso X, Prayer Books, donated by Elisabeth "la Católica"); 94 of don Pedro Ponce, Bishop of Plasencia; 234 from the historian of Aragón, Jerónimo de Zurita; 87 from doctor Juan Páez de Castro; 293 from Mallorca, Barcelona and the Monasteries of La Murta and Poblet, the majority being the works of Raimundo Lull or Lulio; 31 more from the Prior of Roncesvalles. 139 prohibited books passed from the Inquisition to the Escorial; 206 from the humanist Benito Arias Montano, organizer of the Library, among which there were 72 Hebrew manuscripts; 486 from the Library of the Marquis of Los Vélez; 935 from the Cardinal of Burgos, don Francisco de Bobadilla y Mendoza; and 135 from the Archbishop of Tarragona, the humanist and numismat don Antonio

Agustín, most of which were Greek manuscripts; not counting many others given by private citizens among whom stand
out don Jorge de Beteta and Dr. Burgos de Paz.

There were more than 10.000 volumes from all these sour-
ces and they were temporarily placed in a chamber which was
later used as a bedroom for the novices. Fray Juan de San
Jerónimo was appointed to gather them together. There they
were arranged and classified by Arias Montano, helped by
Fr. Juan and the Padre José Sigüenza who later remained as
librarian. By command of the King they were transferred in
1577 to what is now called the high library whilst the magnificent rooms where they were to be permanently located were
completed. These were ready in 1593. Padre Sigüenza gathered all the printed volumes in the Main Hall and the manuscripts in the adjoining room, occupying almost half of the north
side of the King's Court, where there was a rich walnut case,
placing the forbidden and duplicated books on the upper part,
as they were used less.

During the time of Philip III important additions were made:
the library of the bibliophile, writer and politician don Alonso
Ramírez de Prado in 1609; in 1614 there was an exceptional
addition of 4.000 selected Arabic manuscrip s which made up
the Library of Mulen Zidan, Sultan of Morocco, when the two
vessels carrying his riches were seized on the Barbary coasts
by Pedro de Lara, captain of the Spanish galleys in the Medi-
terranean. The greater part of the Library belonging to the
Conde Duque de Olivares also found its way into El Escorial
during the reign of Philip IV.

Philip II knew that these centres needed a fixed rent for
their upkeep and increase, and this he granted in 1573. These
rents were increased by his successors and, by the time of
Philip IV, it amounted to some 2.000 ducats. "With such pro-

tection and so many elements, the Library of El Escorial should be the first in Europe, not only in the number of its books, but also in their selection and merit". But this was not the case, for often the rent went to things other than the Library and at other times the lack of sensibility and wrong judgement hurt the books and their richness. It also suffered misfortunes which maimed its collections. In 1671 a terrible fire destroyed more than 4.000 manuscripts and many printed volumes; similarly, it suffered greatly in the Napoleonic invasion, and between the years 1820-1823. Today, there are preserved some 40.000 printed volumes in the Library; 2.000 Arabic manuscripts, more than 2.000 in Latin and as many in other languages, 580 in Greek and 72 in Hebrew. In spite of the losses suffered, the whole is of priceless worth, and forms one of the most valued collections in the world.

By the wish of the Spanish monarchs, and in particular of a great one, a *Library* was constructed ex profeso for the first time.

It is situated above the portal leading into the Court of Kings, on the right of which is the entrance and staircase which leads to it. The entrance is in the angle formed by the small cloisters on the third floor between the north and the west. Its entrance is through a beautiful portal whose centre occupies the door, flanked by two pedestals with their corresponding spiral column which supports the cornice with an open frontispiece. A feigned black plaque is installed here with an inscription which threatens excommunication to anyone who removes books or other objects from the Library. The entire façade is fashioned from fine woods, beautifully and artistically assembled. Through this door one enters the Library which consists of a spacious room 54 by 9 metres, with the paving made from white and grey marble. It is covered with a cannon vaulted ceiling (10 metres high) with lunettes and it receives plenty of light through five windows and a further five balconies which open into the King's Court and seven great sets of windows which look out over the Lonja to the West.

Around the room have been installed the collection of bookshelves, designed by Juan de Herrera, Tuscan in style; very elegant and beautiful, they are all made from fine woods (like the entrance door), mahogany, walnut, ebony, cedar, terebinth, box-wood and orange-wood. They were carved by the Italian Giuseppe Flecha, assisted by the Spaniards Gamboa, Serrano and others; the cases stand on a small pedestal (30 cms.), in blood-red jasper; the bookcases are fitted between two pedestals with Tuscan columns, and architrave, frieze and cornice; and on top there is a podium divided up by little pilasters which finish in a globe. Originally the books were placed inside standing upright but with the gold edge facing outwards, displaying the title which was engraved thereon, and they remain that way, producing all together a warn tone of attenuated brilliance, singularly attractive.

Two prominent arches with their corresponding pillars divide the room up into three parts. Between the columns of the bookshelves which are divided up by the forementioned pilasters, there are, arranged in similar panels, two on the left and two on the right (as you go in), four portraits full-length and life-size; there is one of *Philip II as an old man* (71 years), a capital work by the painter from Madrid, Juan Pantoja de la Cruz (1551-1610) **(p. 178-179);** opposite is the one of the *Emperor Charles V* (aged 49 years), a most faithful copy of the original by Titian which was lost, by the same master from Madrid (signed in 1609); to his craftsmanship we owe also the portrait of *Philip III* (aged 23 years) on the same side; opposite, *Charles II* aged 14 years, by another Court painter Juan Carreño

Miranda (1614-1685). Over the furniture which houses the coins, fashioned in the Eighteenth Century (2.200 coins) is the portrait of the first historian of El Escorial, Fr. José de Sigüenza, who was also the inventor of the allegories and other subjects on the vaulted roof, also together with Fr. Juan de San Jerónimo and Benito Arias Montano (first classifier and orderer), an important librarian; in the same canvas on the west wall, between windows, may also be found the portraits of Arias Montano and Francisco Pérez Bayer, Latinist and tutor to the Infante sons of Charles III. There is a Roman bust found during the Eighteenth Century excavations at Herculaneum; and two sclagiola reliefs showing reproductions of the face and back of the medal which Jacome Trezzo carved of the architect Juan de Herrera.

From the end of the bookcase the whole of the wall and vaulted ceiling are painted with frescoes with great allegories of the arts and sciences to the cultivation of which the Library was destined. The ceiling is divided into seven parts in which are represented the seven Liberal Arts in the form of matrons: Grammar, Rhetoric, Dialectic, Arithmetic, Music, Geometry and Astronomy, Peregrín Tibaldi carried out here one of his greatest works. In the wall space between the cornice and the bookcases are painted a further 14 stories, two in each division of the ceiling, depicting scenes with each of the arts which have been mentioned, forming a true frieze around the room (2,25 metres high); above it runs a great gilded cornice the adornments of which are marked out with monochrome designs; the two pointed arches on the fore-part were reserved for the principal sciences which embrace all human knowledge: lst those acquired through study, and 2nd, those revealed, Philosophy (north side) and Theology (south side) with their corresponding stories in the frieze: the School of Athens and the Council of Nicaea respectively. The painting of Renaissance grotesques fills in the dividing lines between scenes and compartments, offering a unique perspective in this most beautiful Room. Tibaldi was helped in these paintings by his disciples, particularly Bartolomé Carducci and the gilder Francisco de Viana. The ceiling was completed in 1592 **(pages 100-101-102)**.

The subjects represented in the frescoes are attributed, as has already been mentioned, to Padre José de Sigüenza, the first historian of El Escorial and the wise selection of these corresponded notably to their artistic execution. Peregrín Tibaldi showed considerable mastery of drawing in his figures of young men which seem to support the architraves or some cloth or circles, protraying very difficult and admirable postures and contractions; and the entire assembly of stories in painted with great force in the mixture of colours.

Explanation of the Paintings in the Library

Entrance or south fore-piece. In the pointed arch is Theology, a young and beautiful matron, on an architectonic background, wearing a royal crown and showing the Holy Scripture to the four doctors of the Latin church, St. Hieronymo, St. Ambrose, St. Agustine and St. Gregory, who accompany her.

Below the cornice is the *Council of Nicaea* (in 325). The bishops are presiding and with them is the Emperor Constantine who throws several papers to the fire. On the floor is Arrio, whose doctrine was condemned. Here the Articles of Faith, the base of Christian Theology were declared.

First division, starting at the entrance. The ascending·order of human knowledge represented on the paintings really

Palacio del siglo XVIII. Oratorio
Palais du XVIIIe siècle. Oratoire
Palace of the XVIIIth Century. Oratory

Palais aus dem XVIII Jahrh. Batzimmer
Palazzo del sec. XVIII. Oratorio
Paço do sèculo XVIII. Oratório

129

Goya: Tapiz: El Baile a orillas del Manzanares
Goya: Tapis: Le bal sur les rives du Manzanares
Goya: Tapestry: The dance on the banks of the Manzanares

Goya: Wandteppich: Der Tanz am Manzanaresufer
Goya: Arazzo: Il ballo alle rive del Manzanare
Goya: Tapête: O baile nas margens do Manzanares

Goya: Tapiz: La riña en la Venta Nueva
Goya: Tapis: La querelle à la Venta Nueva
Goya: Tapestry: The Fight in the New Inn

Goya: Wandteppich: Der Striet in der neuen Kneipe
Goya: Arazzo: La rissa alla taverna Nuova
Goya: Tapête: A rixa na Estalagem Nova

Goya: Tapiz: La cometa, siglo XVIII
Goya: Tapis: Le cerf-volant, XVIIIe siècle
Goya: Tapestry: The Kite, XVIIIth century

Goya: Wandteppich: Der Papierdrache, XVIII Jahrh
Goya: Arazzo: La Cometa, sec. XVIII
Goya: Tapète: Oa papagaio, S. XVIII

Goya: Tapiz: El cacharrero, siglo XVIII
Goya: Tapis: Le potier, XVIIIᵉ siècle
Goya: Tapestry: The Pottery Seller, XVIIIth century

Goya: Wandteppich: Der Toepfer, XVIII Jahrh
Goya: Arazzo: Il venditore di cocci, sec. XVIII
Goya: Tapête: O loiceiro, S. XVIII

Goya: Tapiz: Las lavanderas, siglo XVIII
Goya: Tapis: Las lavandières, XVIIIe siècle
Goya: Tapestry: The Washerwomen, XVIIIth century

Goya: Wandteppich: Die Waschfrauen, XVIII Jahrh
Goya: Arazzo: Le lavandaie, sec. XVIII
Goya: Tapête: As lavadeiras, S. XVIII

Goya: Tapiz: Muchachos subiendo a un árbol
Goya: Tapis: Enfants grimpant sur un arbre
Goya: Tapestry: Boys climbing a tree

Goya: Wandteppich: Knaben auf einen Baum kletternd
Goya: Arazzo: Ragazzi che salgono su un albero
Goya: Tapête: Rapaces subindo a uma àrvore

Despacho del Rey   Arbeitszimmer des Koenigs
Bureau du Roi   Studio del Re
The King´s Office   Escritório do Rei

begins from the north fore-piece with Philosophy, but tourist visits and explanations reverse this order thus inverting the description.

On the vaulted ceiling, *Astronomy* reclines on a celestial globe and several children around her study the course of the heavenly bodies. In the left hand recess are painted Ptolemy and Alphonse X, "El Sabio", King of Castile; opposite, Euclid and Juan Sacrobocco, eminent astronomers.

On the left, below the cornice, is representd the supernatural eclipse which occured at the time of Christ's Crucifixion; St. Dionisius Areopagitas, Apolophanes, who caused the conversion of the former.

In front is King Hezekiah in bed, gravely ill, and the prophet Isaias who promises him, in the name of God, fifteen more years of life; as a guarantee of the promise he shows him a solar quadrant whose shadow recedes ten degrees.

Second Division. Geometry on the ceiling with a compass in her hand and several children around her. In the left-hand recess are Archimedes and Johan Muller of Monterregio and on the right Pythagoras and Aristarchus. In the stripe that separates this science from the preceding one are painted Dicareus Siculus and Cirengus.

Beneath the cornice, on the left, Egyptian priests mark out the boundaries of the lands which have been obliterated by the floods of the Nile; on the other side Archimedes, who is absorbed in solving a geometrical problem, does not realize that the Roman soldiers have entered Syracuse by assault and these soldiers kill him.

Third division. In the vaulted ceiling, playing the lyre, Music with various children. In the lefthand recess, Tubal and Pythagoras; and opposite, Anfion and Orpheus.

Beneath the cornice, on the right. Orpheus takes out his wife, Eurycides, of Hell having made Cerberus fall asleep beforehand with the music from his lyre; and in front, David, who, playing his harp, appeases the anger of King Saul.

Fourth division. Arithmetic on the ceiling accompanied by various youngsters who hold tablets with numbers.

In the right-hand recess, Jordan and Xenocrates; Arquitas Tarentinus and Boetius on the other side.

Beneath the cornice, on the right, many Gimnosophist philosophers naked, discuss the numbers; in front, the Queen of Sheba listens and presents enigmas to Solomon.

Fifth division. On the ceiling, *Dialectic,* a figure in a difficult posture, crowned by half a moon symbolizing the *horned arguments* of the Latins or the *dilemma* of the Greeks, accompanied by various youngsters. In the right-hand recess Pythagoras and the philosopher Origenes; opposite, Zenon and Meliso.

Below the cornice on the right-hand side, St. Ambrose and St. Augustine arguing and St. Monica kneeling to implore the Conversion of her son; opposite, the philosopher Zenon of Elea, founder of Dialictics points out to some young men two doorways depicting Truth and Falsity, thus establishing the criterion of the senses.

On the arc and belt which separate this science from the following one are painted, on the left, Pindarus and Horace, with Homer and Virgil opposite.

Sixth division. On the ceiling, *Rhetoric* with a caduceus in one hand and at her side several children and a lion.

In the right-hand recess, Hercules of Gaul, with a stick in his hand, and with little chains of gold and silver coming out of a mouth, finishing with the ears of various men who are listening to him thus representing the power of eloquence; in front, Cicero saves Caius Rabirius, accused of a capital crime for having killed the evil Saturnine.

Between the two arcs which separate this division from the following one, are represented Plinius and Titus Livius in the middle of elegant grotesques.

Seventh division. On the ceiling, *Grammar* with a garland in her hand and some lashes in the other, accompanied by various graceful children with their books and notebooks.

In the left-hand recess Marcus Terentius Varron and Sixtus Pompeius; opposite, Tiberius Donatus and Antonio de Nebrija.

Beneath the cornice, on the right, the first school of grammar in Babylon; on the left, the construction of the Tower of Babel, where different languages originated.

The centre of the room is decorated with an armillary sphere and five grey marble tables from the time of Philip II, between which are two octagonal porphyry stands, a present from Philip IV; the tables, in their lower part also contains books and the upper part has been fixed with showcases where the most valuble codices in the Library are exhibited, such as some of the books of Alphonse, "El Sabio"; the *Cantiges of St. Mary; The Book of Games; the Lapidary,* all of them from the Thirteenth Century; several *autobiographical works* of St. Teresa of Jesús, *Breviaries* of the Catholic Monarchs, Charles V **(p. 99)** and of Philip II, the last two pieces from El Escorial workshop, as well as a *Prayer Book;* notable examples of Mozarabic codices, Castilian school of great originality because of its expression and force; such as two *Conciliar Codices;* the *Albedense* and the *Emilianense* both from the Tenth Century; and an *Explanation of the Apocalypse of St. John by St. Beato de Liébana,* Eleventh Century; the *Trojan Chronicle* and the *Ordaining of Alcalá,* both from the Fourteenth Century, outstanding examples of Castilian miniatures, the latter belonged to Pedro I, el Cruel; the *Virgilian Codice (Aenead),* an admirable example of Italian

Renaissance miniatures; the *Book of Designs* of Francisco de
Holanda, XVIth Century, which has reproductions of monuments
and other antiques of Rome and Italy. The *Aureus Codex* with
gilded letters which contains the Gospels, a work of the Monastery of Reichenau, Germany (XIth Century); *The Apocalypsis*
coming from the House of Savoy (XIIIth Century); a precious
collection of Prayer Books- from the XVth and XVIth Centuries
in Flemish and French art; a collection of Byzantine codices,
and other very notable Persian and Arabic manuscripts among
which a *Koran* that belonged to the King of Barbary, Muley
Zidán, stands out. The collection of bindings, both Spanish and
foreign, is also outstanding. Its installation on elegantly designed cabinets, the allegorical paintings on the ceiling, the
pictures and other complementary objects (showcases, armillary spheres, busts, medals), constituted a new kind of Library
in its time, which was afterwards imitated by all the successive
great royal libraries in Europe.

The so called *Library of Manuscripts* was located above the
main one and it was poorer in its adornments. Since fires were
feared, the books, together with the book-shelves, were taken
to a wide hall which comes out to the Patio de los Reyes, in
which are kept bibliographic riches of incalculable value.

The Palaces

Right from the time when the Monastery was built, a quarter of the building was destined to be used as apartments for
the royal family and their retinue. This part stretches from the
middle of the northern side to the middle of the eastern side
as well as the whole of the projecting body which surrounds
the main chapel; this section is known as the *Apartments of
Philip II* and is what is properly called the *Palace*.

The Austrias made of El Escorial the Royal Site "par excellence". The monarchs and their court spent long periods of time there in great pomp and splendour, organizing feasts and merriments typical of courtly life. With the advent of the Bourbons, La Granja, El Pardo and Aranjuez, besides El Escorial, had to share in lodging the royalty and their retinue. A fondness for hunting, so abundant in the mountains of El Escorial, led Charles III and his son, Charles IV. once again to the monasterial Palace, which they restored, decorated and furnished in great richness; Charles IV commissioned his architect, Juan de Villanueva, to build the present staircase.

The collection of furniture, silk tapestry, clocks, candelabra and chandeliers is outstanding; but what is most important to be admired in the Palace is the splendid collection of more than 200 tapestries, most of them from the Royal Factory of St. Barbara in Madrid, which adorn the walls of the apartments, affording them a note of richness and grace with their cheerful colours, depicting popular scenes, most of them by Goya, Bayeu and Castillo, genuinely Spanish, and the graceful Flemish ones by Teniers or Wouwerman.

Many of the ceilings painted by Felipe López are in Pompeian style, so much in the taste of the Imperial epoch. The series of rooms decorated in this way, with their white and gold furniture, or of mahogany with gilded bronze apliques, drapes and tapestries harmonizing with them, their clocks, candelabra, vases, and porcelain from the Buen retiro, etc., are of an extraordinarily pleasant attractiveness and constitute an exact and authentic model in every element of the time of Ferdinand VII (Imperial).

Palace of the Bourbons

The entrance to the Palace is through the centre of the northern façade **(p. 18)** (ticket office), followed by a staircase made by the architect Villanueva in the XVIIIth Century, where several paintings are displayed; the best of these are *Apollo Flaying the Satyr Marcias,* and *Arachne and the Goddess Pallas,* both by Lucas Jordán, some *flower pieces* by Seghers and several *landscapes* by different artists.

Following that, there are three antechambers with beautiful neo-classical and Imperial furniture and some romantic "cathedral" pictures and prints, clocks and candelabra, which open the way into the Palace of the Bourbons. We shall mention the most interesting paintings, such as the full colour copies of the *Lodges of the Vatican* decorated by Raphael, and *Vatican Museums* in the cornices (the little entrance apartment); *Adoration of the Kings,* in the style of A. Vaccaro; *Birth of the Virgin* and her *presentation in the Temple,* both from the school of Andrea del Sarto; *The Immaculate,* a Murillesque bust; *Virgin with the Child who is playing with a rosary,* by Artemisa Lomi, called Gentillleschi (XVIIIth Century); and *portrait of the Infanta María Carolina Fernanda, as a child* (with her hat in hand), by Francisco Lacoma (XIXth Century).

Second antechamber: Portraits of the kings *Charles IV* with his wife *María Luisa,* copies of Goya; four *busts of ladies* by Rosalva Carriera (1672-1757), and *Portrait of the Prince of Capua,* as a child (copying a bust) by F. Lacoma.

The following room is known as *"el chinero"* (the china closet), because in it are kept and displayed pieces of China, that is to say, valuable examples of porcelains from China, Saxony, Sèvres and Buen Retiro. A collection of *still life* pain-

tings adorn its walls —still-life paintings by López Enguidanos;
Hunting Scene, a copy of Martín de Vos and a *Pelican,* a copy
of a wood painting by A. Durero. The group of rooms visited
next are the so called *King's* Rooms (Charles IV) and are the
rooms which were used for official matters. They start with
the formal *Dining Hall,* a spacious room with a splendid
collection of tapestries by the Court painters: Goya, Bayeu,
Castillo and Anglois **(p. 114).** The ones by Goya are: *The
Woodcutters,* woven in 1789; *The Dance on the Banks of the
Manzanares,* woven in 1788 **(p. 130),** those by Bayeu are:
*Lunch in the Country; Flower Girl; The Horchata Maker; Lunch
in the Chandler's Shop; and the Bridge of St. Isabel.* By Castillo, there is: *El Paseo de las Delicias;* by G. Anglois (imitation
of Wauwerman): *The Flemish Soldier* and *the Farrier;* and by
Teniers: *Children playing chito* and *The Blind Man and his
Guide.* The chairs are Empire style, upholstered with crimson
damask; there are clocks and cut-glass chandeliers.

Following it is a small room with tapestries over cartoons
imitated from Teniers and Wouwerman with scenes of Flemish
soldiers. After that is the *Ambassadors' Anteroom* **(p. 115)**
with a beautiful collection of tapestries over cartoons by
Goya: The *Maja and the Cloaked Men; The Kite,* painted in
1778 **(p. 132);** *Boys picking fruits,* painted in 1777 **(p.
135);** *The Pottery Seller,* woven in 1781 **(p. 133);** *The
Child in the Tree,* painted in 1779; *The Swing bar,* painted
in 1778; *The Washerwomen,* woven in 1789 **(p. 134);**
The Gigantillas, woven in 1793. Belonging to Bayeu: *The Card
Players,* and to Castillo: *The Paseo de las Delicias.* There are
Imperial style chairs upholstered in yellow satin and three
tables, two of serpentine marble and one of jasper with clocks
and Sèvres vases.

The *Hall of Ambassadors* **(p. 118)** is another of the most beautiful rooms in the Palace of the XVIIIth Century, also enriched with a collection of beautiful Bayeu tapestries: *Christmas Nigth; The Game with the Little Cow* **(p. 120);** *The Inn; The Gardener; The Game of Bochas* **(p. 119);** *The Card Game* and *The Sausage-maker, Pedro Rico* born in Candelario (Salamanca), who was sausage maker to the king Charles IV. It has Imperial style furniture and chairs upholstered in white silk; Sèvres vases; and clocks. The ceiling was painted by Felipe López.

The small room called the *Hall of the Oratory,* as there is one in it, displays tapestries which depict *scenes from the adventures of Telemachus,* from sketches by Rubens (?), woven in the Royal Factory in Madrid; the encounter of the shipwrecked Telemachus and Mentor with the nymph Calipso on the beach of her island (now cut into two) was woven from drawings by the Royal Painter under Philip V, Michael Angel Houasse, in 1734. The furniture is Imperial style and the chairs are upholstered in blue silk. The ivory bas-relief depicting the *Baptism of Jesus,* located in the oratory is outstanding.

All the rooms described receive light from the Palace Courtyard and correspond to the north side; leaving the *Room of the Oratory* there follow the rooms called the *Queen's Aparts ments* (María Luisa, wife of Charles IV) and these correspond to the eastern side, also receiving their light from the courtyard through great balconies.

The first Room is the one with tapestries, made from drawings attributed to Rubens *(Rubens Room)* **(p. 146)** with scenes from the *Adventures of Telemachus,* son of Ulysses, according to the story by Fenelon. That of *Neptune,* with whom the nymph Calipso appears, calming the tempest in which Telemachus and Mentor are going to capsize, was woven in the Low Countries in the

Rincón del Salón Pompeyano
Un côté du Salón Pompeïen
Corner of the Pompeian Salon

Der Pompejanische Saal
Angolo del Salone Pompeiano
Recanto do Salão Pompeiano

145

Antedormitorio primero
Premiere antichambre
First antedormitory

Das erste Vorzimmer
Prima Anticamera del Dormitorio
Primeira antecâmara

146

Perspectiva de la batalla de Higueruela
Perspective de la bataille de Higueruela
View of the battle of Higueruela

Die Schlacht von Higueruela
Prospettiva della battaglia di Higueruela
Perspectiva da batalha de Higueruela

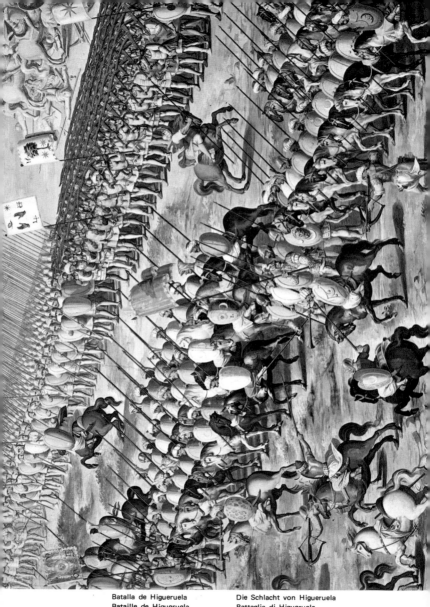

Batalla de Higueruela
Bataille de Higueruela
Battle of Higueruela

Die Schlacht von Higueruela
Battaglia di Higueruela
Batalha de Higueruela

Salón de Honor Ehrensaal
Salon d´Honneur Salone d´Onore
Hall of Honour Salão de Honra

Pinacoteca. Escuelas italianas
Pinacothèque. Ecoles Italiennes
Pinacotheca. Italian Schools

Bildergallerie. Italienische Schulen
Pinacoteca. Scuole Italiane
Pinacoteca. Escolas Italianas

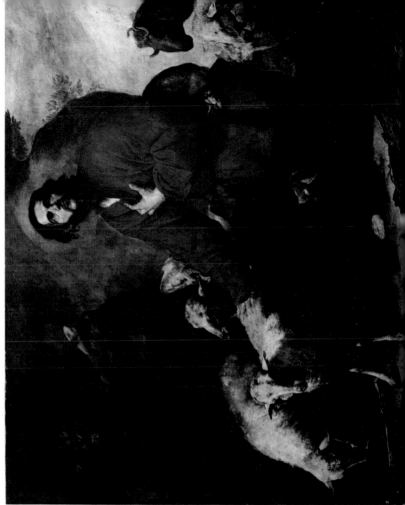

Ribera: José guardando los ganados de Labán
Ribera: Joseph gardant les troupeaux de Labán
Ribera: Joseph grazing the Flock from Labán

Ribera: Joseph behuetend die Herden Labans
Ribera: Giussepe guardando gli allevamenti di Labán
Ribera: José guardando o gado de Labán

Velázquez: La Túnica de José
Velázquez: La tunique de Joseph
Velázquez: Joseph´s tunic

Velázquez: Tunike des Joseph
Velázquez: La tunica di Giussepe
Velázquez: A túnica de José

XVIIth Century, by Urbano Leynier, from Brussels (1674-1747);
the rest, from the Madrid Factory of St. Barbara, are from cartoons by the French painter Houasse, as has been previously
mentioned. The tapestries over the doors, *Dead Birds* and
Wild Boar, are by Bayeu; the furniture is imperial; chairs and
cupboards are upholstered in crimson silk; above a bureau there
is a group of biscuit porcelain, made in the factory of Capodi-
monte, Naples, In 1781, and which depicts a Boar Hunt atten-
ded by King Ferdinand IV of Naples, his wife Caroline and other
personages, a present offered in 1782 to Charles IV of Spain,
at that time Prince of Asturias. The ceiling was painted by Felipe López.

The following room is decorated with Anglois tapestries in
imitation of Wouwerman, and the subjects are *hunting* scenes;
over the doors there is a *Fox eating a rabbit,* and an *Eagle cla-
wing a hare,* all these works having come from the Royal
Factory in Madrid. The chairs are in English style, upholstered
in white silk.

The *Pompeian* style room **(p. 145),** so called because of
the beautiful tapestries which adorn it, in which great female
figures stand out like cameos. In the one of the wall above the
mantelpiece, two of these figures can be admired, so well executed that they appear to be in relief. They were woven in the
Factory of St. Barbara in Madrid, from cartoons by José Castillo at the end of the XVIIIth Century. The Imperial chairs and
cupboards are upholstered in crimson satin; on one of the
tables there is a beautiful alabaster and bronze clock, with
Psyche and Love.

Then comes another important room whit the *Tapestries of
Goya: The Fight in the New Inn,* one the most outstanding,
painted in 1791 **(p. 131);** and *The Child with the Bird,*
painted in 1779. Other tapestries are: *The Piper,* by an unk-

nown artist; *The Fishermen; The Hunters; The Garden on
the Island of Aranjuez* and *The Bull fastened with a Rope* are
all by Bayeu. The chairs are neo-classical and the curtains are
made of sky-blue silk.

A small room with small tapestries depicting hunting scenes
over the doors, leads into the last Room of the XVIIIth Century
Palace; the one with Tapestries by Teniers, imitations executed
by the Royal Factory in Madrid, such as *The Game of Bowls, The
Game of Cards, The Drinkers, The Pipe Smokers* and *Three Pea-
sants*. By Goya: *Hunting Dogs* (over the door). Imperial style
chairs.

Parallel to the rooms just described, but receiving its light
from the eastern side, are found the private appartments of the
Kings and, attached to them, the rooms located on the same
floor of the north eastern part, in the square angle formed by
the West and North wall stretches which constitute one of the
most splendid groups to be admired in the Palace. They are the
so-called *Rooms of Fine Woods,* which can be visited with special tickets. This visit begins with the room of the tapestry of
Telemachus and from thence one enters the *Reception Room,*
with furniture of romantic «cathedral» style in white with
yellow silk upholstery; the mantlepiece is black marble and the
chandelier is bronze and glass; the ceiling is by Felipe López.
Various tapestries adorn this room, among which stand out
The Flower Girl, the Bridge over the Canal, by Bayeu, and *Hunting Scenes with a falcon* by Teniers. From this room, and
wearing slippers, one can visit the *Rooms of Fine Woods,* so-
called because their floors, doors, shutters and windows, friezes and moundings constitute a delicate and exquisite inlay
and cabinet work. The woods are hurandy, pará, lapacho, black
and yellow palosanto, laurel, cedar, ebony, terebinth. The work
was begun in the time of Charles IV (who was very fond of

cabinet work and circumvolution) and was finished in 1831, under the direction of the Royal cabinet maker Angel Maeso; in them one can admire landscapes, vases with flowers, bows, drapery, stars, Greek urns, and adornments of all kinds with an extremely rich ensemble of exquisite taste; it cost 28 million reales, a considerable sum at that time.

The ironwork of all the doors and windows was the work of Ignacio Millán, the palace master locksmith; the work is of inlaid gold in gilt iron, similar to those of Toledo and Eibar, executed with exquisite minuteness.

The rooms are arranged in the following order: *the office* **(p. 136);** *the toilet room; the anteoratory;* and *the oratory* **(p. 129)** standing out in the latter is the despatch table, extremely exquisite, and with precious reliefs in gilt bronze with historical scenes from Spanish history —the Surrender of Granada— and the stools are also of exquisite cabinet work; the upholstery is the same as that of the hangings in the rooms, in rich silk and gold cloth; the office (the most luxurious of all) is in sky-blue silk; the dressing room is in orange silk; the anteoratory with embroidery on a yellow background; and the oratory, in white, embroidered with gold and green, in a vine-leaf design. Maella painted the ceilings except for the anteoratory one which is the work of Juan Gálvez.

Returning to the *Antechamber or Reception Hall,* one may then visit the rest of the rooms which are: a small Pompeian style room with neo-classical Charles IV chairs and two small lacquered Philippine scissor chairs; the *Queen's bedroom* with the bed and chairs in the Imperial style; tapestry of *The old bull-ring;* the *Queen's dressing room* with the *Game of Pelota* tapestry by Goya; to the side, a toilet room with the bowl incrusted with gold, forming the ornament; the *King's bedroom* (Charles IV); neoclassical bed and dressing room with a washstand; tapestries of the *Street of Alcalá* and the *dance of the Chisperos* by Bayeu; *the daily dining room* with a tapestry of the *Game of Pelota* by Goya; *the music room* (because of the neoclassical piano which is displayed in it); Imperial furniture, braziers with a stand similar to those in the *Hall of the Ambassadors,* a lamp table, also Imperial, which supports a glass engraved templet, tapestries by Bayeu: *The Game of Bowls* (2nd tapestry) and the *Card Players;* by Anglois; *The Shepherd* and *The Blacksmith;* and by Teniers: *The Vintage.*

Hall of Battles

After the visit to the Palace one may continue into a beautiful hall 55 by 5 metres and 7 metres high, the *Hall of Battles* **(p. 147-8),** because in it are represented in frescoe paintings, the most famous battles won by the Castilian and Spanish troops in different epochs; in the south canvas is the *Battle of Higueruela* won by John II of Castile over the Moors of Granada in the Sierra Elvira in the year 1431, according to an ancient drawing which was found in the Alcázar of Segovia (1587) and which, when shown to Philip II, was commissioned to be faithfully reproduced; it covers several episodes of the battle: the king of Castile's camp with his tents and trenches; the enemy troops in line of battle, standing out in the Castilian one King John and the Constable don Alvaro de Luna, his favourite; the bloody clash of the two armies and, finally, the Granada army in complete defeat and disarray: the Castilians penetrate further into the suburbs of Granada where all is confusion and horror, the Moorish women fleeing from them with their children (Granelo, Castello and Tavarón). In both foreparts were painted the two expeditions which the armada of Philip II carried out

with great success in the Third Islands or the Azores (Granelo);
on the northern side, between the ten windows, are represented various episodes of the Battle and Taking of San Quintín (Fabricio Castello) and of other fortresses in France, Flanders and Portugal and a review of the troops in Cantillana by
Philip II in 1580. Its authors were, as has been mentioned,
Nicolás Granelo and Fabricio Castello, sons of the Bergamasco,
and Lázaro Tavarón and Orazio Cambiasso, son of Lucas, who
painted in Renaissance grotesques. The room was restored
between 1882 and 1889, by Rudesindo Marín and his sons
Manuel and Mariano and in 1890 the iron railing was placed
there, a sketch by the architect José de Lama.

XVIth Century Palace

Contrasted with the grandiose nature of the Monastery and
the richness of the Bourbon Palace, is the modesty of the
XVIth Century Palace, where the Founder King lived and died.
Its rooms are distributed around the Main Chapel of the church
and around a central courtyard, in Doric style, called the *Courtyard of the Masks,* because of two fountains on its eastern
side which spout water through two stone masks; the architectonic ensemble froms the so-called *gridiron's handle,* as the
plan of El Escorial is commonly called. The rooms may be grouped into three: *the Apartments of the Infanta Isabel Clara Eugenia, The throne Room* with its antechambers and adjoining
rooms and the *Apartments of Philip II.* They all remained empty
during the XVIIIth and XIXth Centuries, but during the second
decade of the present century they were faithfylly restored,
preserving their original arrangement; in them are several
works of art, furniture of the time, as well as personal posse-

ssions of the Prudent King, powerfully reminiscent and which help to awake in the visitor the awareness of the severe greatness of their original agrarious inhabitants.

Descending from the *Hall of Battles* down a stone staircase and crossing a cloister or gallery decorated with oil paintings by Fabricio Castello with the family trees of the kings of the House of Austria and others by Pantoja de la Cruz representing groups of the families of Charles V and Philip II praying, earlier than the bronze ones on the Main Altar, and different from them, one reaches the rooms which were at first called the Apartment of the Queen, and which are known today as the Apartments of Princess Isabel Clara Eugenia, favourite daughter of Philip II, later governess of the Low Countries. Along the north side there is a room with windows overlooking the gardens **(p. 177)** where the inside bedrooms or apartments open; at the back of it there are two oratories of beautiful marble which connect with the presbytery and could be used on certain occasions as a private tribune. In the bedroom of Isabel Clara Eugenia, one may admire a walnut bed with canopy and curtains in Oriental Style (XVIth Century), probably from the Philippines or the Goa Indies, as well as some furniture of the time, among which stands out a clavichord which belonged to Charles V; an ivory Christ by Alonso Cano and, on a little walnut table, a wax Nativity representing the *Adoration of the Kings (Magi),* and various little pictures in hammered bronze with mystical subjects. Various pictures adorn the walls, and, among the most notable, one must mention a triptych of the *Virgin with Child surrounded by Saints and musical angels,* school of Cologne; the portraits of the Infantas *Isabel Clara Eugenia,* by Bartolomé González, and *Catalina Micaela,* anonymous from the XVIth Century Spanish school, daughters of Philip II; *a full face portrait of that Monarch, as an old man,* attributed to Sánchez Coello (?); the *Archangel St. Michael* (standing and wounding the devil with a lance) a wood painting of the German School (?); *portrait of a writer* (seated at a table with an open book); triptych of the Cologne School (?); the *Virgin seated,* reading in front of a fountain with her blessed companions and musical angels, and as a background a great Gothic facade (centre); *St. Agnes* with various Saints (right); *Donor* with various Saints (left), both doors with a background of tall cypresses **(p. 165);** the *Holy Family,* Italian School; *Virgin with the Child in her Arms,* with a Flemish landscape as background **(p. 163);** *Virgin with the Child, crowned by angels,* both of the Flemish School; *The Calvary* (Christ between the two robbers with the Virgin, St. John and the Marys at the foot of the Cross and two soldiers playing with the Saviour's tunic), is one of the most outstanding and beautiful examples from the collection by Frans Floris (Francisco de Vriend Floris, 1516-1570). Two vellums with the *Assumption of the Virgin* and *San Lorenzo in the gridiron* of liturgical books from the Monastery's workshop, made in miniature by its best maestros, the monks Fr. Andrés de León († 1580) and Fr. Julián de la Fuente el Saz; *miniature portrait of Doña Juana,* sister of Philip II, by Sánchez Coello; *Holy Family with the little St. Johns,* Italian School; *Adoration of the Kings* (wood painting), by Benvenuto Garofalo (1491-1559); *Annunciation and St. Peter* (copper); *the Descent* (the Virgin supports in her lap the body of her dead Son, and she is surrounded by St. John, Joseph of Arimathea and the Marys). In the little room, another *Virgin with Child,* the *Prayer in the Garden,* xvth Century Spanish school; *St. Elizabeth and St. John the Baptist as a child* (and an angel with a palm and a lamb on the left, allusive to both).

The Apartments of Philip II

Following through these apartments of the Infanta Isabel Clara Eugenia, there continues a passage which goes over the ceiling of the Pantheon of the Kings and then behind the High Altar to reach the *Apartments of Philip II,* which correspond to the southern side; it is shaped like a square, 9 metres on each side, divided in length by a partition into almost two equal parts; the inside is similarly divided by another perpendicular partition, the first one being separated into two small rooms; one of them is the bedroom with a door leading into the church; thus, from his bed, the king could follow the cults and various positions of the officiant, as can be appreciated in the original drawing by Juan de Herrera which is on display in this very room; in it is preserved the bed with canopy and curtains and a spout of holy water bearing the bronze monogram of Philip II; the ensemble is completed with a pair of armchairs, several small pictures of religious subjects and the floor is covered with a rug or carpet made of leather. The great king died in this room on the 13th of September, 1958.

Connecting the bedroom with the office there is a small room with an altar, and on it is an old copy of *Christ Bearing the Cross,* by Titian.

The large room **(p. 180-1),** outside, nearly 5 metres wide, receives light through three large windows at floor level. The paving is brick, the walls and ceiling are painted white and a high socle from Talavera is its only adornment; it served as on office for the king; the table, the portfolio and the autograph, various upright armchairs with a ramrod for his injured leg and the bookcase with his favourite books, are the personal souvenirs of the glorious monarch. On the walls are displayed

Museo de Arquitectura. Las máquinas
Musée d´Architecture. Les Machines
Museum of Architecture. Machines

Architekturmuseum. Die Maschinen
Museo d´Architettura. La macchine
Museu de Arquitectura. As máquinas

Roger Van der Weyden: Calvario
Roger Van der Weyden: Calvaire
Roger Van der Weyden: Calvary

Roger Van der Weyden: Golgatha
Roger Van der Weyden: Calvario
Roger Van der Weyden: Calvário

Virgen con el Niño. Escuela flamenca, siglo XVI   Jungfrau mit dem Kind. Flaemische Schule, XVI Jahrh
Vierge à l'enfant. Ecole flamande, XVIe siècle   Vergine col Bambino. Scuola flaminga, Sec. XVI
Virgin with the Child. Flemish Scool, XVIth century   Virgem com o Menino. Escola flamenga, S. XVI

Joaquin Patinir: San Cristóbal
Joaquin Patinir: Saint Christophe
Joaquin Patinir: St. Christopher

Joaquin Patinir: Der Hl. Christoph
Joaquin Patinir: San Cristoforo
Joaquin Patinir: São Cristovao

Escuela de Malinas: La Virgen con el Niño
Ecole de Malines: Vierge à l'Enfant
School of Malinas: The Virgin with the Child

Schule von Mecheln. Die Jungfrau mit dem Kind
Scuola di Malinas. La Vergine col Bambino
Escola de Malinas. A Virgem com o Menino

El Greco: Martirio de San Mauricio
Le Greco: Martyre de Saint Maurice
The Greco: Martyrdom of St. Maurice

Der Greco: Märtyrertum des Hl. Maurizius
Il Greco: Martirio di San Maurizio
O Greco: Martirio de São Maurício

El Greco: Adoración del Nombre de Jesús
Le Greco: Adoration du Nom de Jésus
The Greco: Adoration of the Name of Jesus

Der Greco: Anbetung des Namens Jesus
Il Greco: Adorazione del Nome di Gesú
O Greco: Adoração do Nome de Jesús

El Greco: San Pedro
Le Greco: Saint Pierre
The Greco: St. Peter

Der Greco: Der Hl. Petrus
Il Greco: San Pietro
O Greco: São Pedro

various pictures, some of great interest, such as el Bosco's triptych, *The Capital Sins*, a replica of the one kept in the Prado; it is also known as the *Hay Cart*, central scene, a title inspired in the words of the Prophet Isaiah *"Omnis Caro Feonum"*, "All flesh is hay and all its glory as a flower in the Field". On the cart ride the wordly pleasures in the figures of a woman richly dressed and a young man playing the lute; the cart is drawn by llons, dogs, wolves, bears and fish, all with human bodies, symbolizing the vices or capital sins; to the cart are arriving the social hierarchies trying to climb up on it; on the left panel is depicted *the original sin and Adam and Eve thrown out of Paradise;* on the right is *Hell* with its horrific torments. There also stands out, though very small in size, a *Descent from the Cross,* by the German Adam Elsheimer (1578-1610); a *Calvary* from the German School, as well as a bust of *St. Elena* (wood painting); *The presentation of the Virgin in the Temple* (wood painting), from the Flemish School (in the foreground St. Joaquín and St. Ann about to climb the staircase which leads to a Gothic temple, in front of which is the Virgin, led by an angel; the portraits of the bust of *Charles V* (armed) and his wife, *Empress Elizabeth,* in their youth, from the German School (wood paintings); a portrait in Courtly dress of *Philip II, as an old man* (Pantoja?); *The Virgin with Child between St. Roque and St. Sebastian,* by Benvenuto Garofalo (1481-1559); a little picture representing the *Nail from Christ's Cross* which was the bit of Constantine's horse, today preserved in Milan, a present from St. Carlos Borromeo to Philip II; *The Transfiguration on Mt. Tabor,* a copy from Raphael; *The Holy Family with little St. John* (watching the sleeping Child); from the Italian School, *the Manger and Choir of angels; St. John the Baptist in the desert* and *Judgement with the Resurrection of the Dead,* wood paintings from the Flemish School.

Anotner corridor leads from the apartments of Philip II to the Throne Room and its adjoining rooms, such as the *Antechamber or Ambassadors Room,* with simple furnishings according to the taste of the time. Various pictures adorn the walls of this room: *Views of Royal Residences and Hunting Lodges* such as El Pardo, Aranjuez, Valsain, El Campillo, Aceca; original engravings by Pedro Perret which depict various parts of the Monastery of El Escorial, sketched by Juan de Herrera, its architect, as well as some of his sketches for the work. As complementary ornaments in the Room there is an armillary sphere, a stone charm found near the Monastery standing upon a pedestal formed by four columns and an entablature, supporting a weight of 5 kilos. Set into the ground is a curious sun dial in slate and bronze with an inscription on a Rococo plaque which reads: "D.O.M. —P. Ioan Wendingen - Ste. Baumgartner - Austr. Wien— Qui navit 17A55" (To God the Omnipotent and Mightiest P. Juan Wendingen from St. Baumgartner, in Vienna, Austria (made it) diligently in the year 1755); on the opposite end an F crowned, of Fernando VI, also in bronze.

The *Throne Room* is a beautiful room 35 metres long; the furniture is modern, but following the taste of the time, mostly including arm chairs upholstered in scarlet velvet with stripes of different materials; the throne's place is in the middle of the back wall in the center of a platform under a canopy and on it an armchair, a copy of the one which belonged to Charles V; on the wall hang two beautiful XVIth Century tapestries; these tapestries were woven in Brussels of wool, silk, silver and gold, a collection of three which is known as the *Awning of Charles V,* but which do not appear to have been woven with this purpose in mind (although they might have later served to form a canopy), since they date from different

times although they were all made during the first part of the
XVIth Century. Only the tapestry which forms the roof of the
canopy, which represents the *Eternal Father with the Holy
Spirit* surrounded by Seraphims, was made by Pedro Pannemaker, the most famous tapestry maker in the city; the drawing
appears to be work of Miguel Coxcie or Coxcyen, who is
recorded as having done several drawings and whose work is
kept in the Monastery since he was the King's painter. The
apparent black tapestry represents the *Christ of Mercy,* Crucifixion between the Virgin and St. John and two angels flying,
as well as two seated figures; Mercy collecting in a chalice the
Blood from the wound in Christ's side; and Justice sheathing
the sword. Its style, the marked Italian influence it displays,
and more so of Raphael's makes one consider the probable
intervention of Bernard Van Orley **(p. 182).** On each side
a further two precious tapestries also from Brussels and from
the XVIth Century, from the collection called *The Spheres;*
here are the *celestial one* and the *armillary,* surrounded by
deities from Mount Olympus, and supported by Hercules and
Atlas respectively. The walls are decorated with a collection of
paintings commemorating the victorious battles for the Spanish
troops in France and Flanders under the reign of Philip II;
among them stand out those dealing with the Battle of San
Quintín, an old copy by the brothers Castello and Granello; a
collection of old maps engraved and coloured decorates the
entire room, forming a uniform band around it; two cabinets,
characteristic Spanish furniture, decorate the lesser fore parts,
the best one has iron work with perforated bronze and its interior is gilded with little columns of Renaissance like architecture, although of a greatly accentuated popular taste. In the
floor a sun dial identical to the one described in the last room
and with equal date. The door leading into the next room is a

beautiful piece of German cabinet-work from the end of the
XVIth Century or the beginning of the XVIIth; an exquisite
workmanship of marketry, in fine woods.

Another adjoining room is now called the *Hall of portraits,*
because of the paintings which predominate there; these are
the portraits of *Charles V* (more than half body, at 47 years of
age), by Pantoja de la Cruz, signed in 1547; of *Philip II* by Antonio Moro (Anton van Darshorst Mor, 1519 (?) - 1576); of *Philip III,* an old copy of Pantoja; *Philip IV as a child,* by Bartolomé
González, signed in 1612; and *Charles II* at the age of 14 years,
by Carreño, all of them full body studies and on foot; the *Infanta Doña Juana,* sister of Philip II, attributed to Sánchez Coello;
Don John of Austria, illegitimate son of the Emperor Charles V,
a copy of A. Moro; and the Duke-General Filiberto of Savoy,
from the XVIth Century Spanish School. The other pictures are:
St. Margaret of Cortona, a copy of Titian (the Saint, full-length,
comes out of the dragon which explodes because of the Cross);
and two pictures with the same subject matter: *The Temptations of St. Anthony,* from the school of Bosch. Among the
furniture are displayed, as curious works, two little chairs where
King Philip II could rest his injured leg.

These apartments end with the so-called *Pedanchair,* as
this is the most notable of their furnishings. This chair was
often used by Philip II to move from Madrid to El Escorial and
in it he made his last journey to die in his monasterial Palace.
The chair was converted into a litter simply by fastening to the
high poles an awning and side curtains either of canvas or leather. This room is decorated with numerous pictures: four works
by Jacopo Bassano: *Adoration of the Shepherds, the Crowning of Thorns, Jesus at the Home of Martha and Mary,* and
Noli Me Tangere; the Descent, from the German school; *David
cutting off Goliath's head,* by Miguel Coxcie; *the Holy Family,*

a copy of Raphael (?); *Allegory of the Arts; the Annunciation* by B. Carducci (?); *the Judgement of Solomon,* a copy of Lucas Jordán; *the Flagellation of the Lord* (Jesus, seated in a large courtyard and with His eyes bound, receives the mockery from various coarse tormentors), by Juan Correa (?), XVIth Century; and the *Marys in the Tomb of Christ,* from the style of C. Veronés **(p. 183).**

The New Museums

These comprise the new installations for the Pinacotheca and the Museum of Architecture.

The Pinacotheca. When the collection of paintings was re-integrated into El Escorial after the foundation, in 1940, of the Patrimonio Nacional, a high governing body which looks after the Palaces and Royal Places, the compelling necessity to undertake works for an adequate installation of the extensive collection of paintings was realized as they had already been deficiently displayed for a long time in the Capitular Halls and in the Sacristy of the Monastery, in which the inadequate and scarce light, as well as the lack of space, damaged not only the contemplation of the pictures, but also impaired the sublime qualities of colour, light and composition of these masterpieces which, completely covered the walls, still with a criterion of the Baroque epoch.

It has now been possible to undertake those works with more powerful means than normal for the maintenance of so great a building, thanks to the tremendous effort exerted and completed in restorations and constructions to achieve the greatest splendour and efficiency in the celebration of the IVth Centenary of the Monastery. Some of the most outstanding are the restoration works of the *Summer Palace of Philip II.* This Palace was left completely abandoned and in considerable ruin, without carpentry and flooring and with its plastering destroyed, despite the attempt at restoration at the beginning of the century by the architect of the Royal House, José María Florit (Andrada).

This Palace coincides in every way with *Philip II's Royal Apartments,* although greatly altered over the ages particularly under Philip IV and even more under Charles II, who possibly altered the staircase which links both the Summer and Winter Palaces, near the rooms which are now called the apartments of the Infanta Isabel Clara Eugenia. The Summer one is on the lower floor on a level with the Jardín de los Frailes, and consists of all the rooms and chambers with their small halls, which coincide exactly with those of the upper floor, or Palace of Philip II, which surround the Courtyard of the Masks and from the "handle of the gridiron" in the plan of the Monastery; the paintings from the Flemish, German, Italian and Spanish Schools have been installed in these rooms **(p. 149-150).**

To this ensemble one must add another two halls, main reception rooms in the time of the Founder, but divided in their height and profusely walled up in the time of Charles IV (1789-1808). Now, all the additions having been destroyed and with a work of restoration of the original structure, these rooms can once more be seen as they were originally designed, with dimensions and aspect similar to the Capitular Halls; like these, they have been plastered in white and grey marble; the doors jambs, also in grey marble, are the old ones. The main hall (16 by 9,50 metres), called the Museum's *rooms of Honour,* has five recessed in the projecting facade, in two heights; the higher ones have upright lunettes cutting the vaulted ceiling with an expert elliptical cannon; from it, through two small doors, one passes into another room of smaller dimensions (7,80 by 9,50 metres) which displays a beautiful vaulted ceiling in a corner of the cloister, with lunettes; it is known as the *Hall of the Grecos.* Returning to the Room of Honour, one finally passes out into the courtyard of the Palace or Chancery.

We shall now describe the contents of the rooms of this new, beautiful Museum, which has endowed Madrid with another first class Pinacotheca.

Room I. Containing XVth and XVIth Century paintings of the Flemish and German School. The main pictures in this room are: *Landscape with St. Christopher,* by Joaquín Patinir (1480-1524) **(p. 164);** *The Creation,* fragment of the *Garden of Las Delicias,* a replica from the wing of the triptych bearing this name in the Prado Museum, by Jerónimo Bosch, el Bosco (1450-62-1516), *The Insults* (Ecce Homo), in the form of a background, also by el Bosco (2nd small room); the *Studies of Natural History,* by Alberto Durero (1471-1528) and the Triptych by Gerard David (1450-60-1523) with *Pity* (Centre), *St. John the Baptist* (Left) and *St. Francis receiving the stigmas* (Right). The rest of the works are: in the first display case, *The Triptych* on parchment in the style of an anonymous miniaturist after the school of G. David, with *St. Hieronymo in Prayer* (centre), the *Flight into Egypt* (left), and *St. Anthony* (right), and *The Temptations of St. Anthony,* from the school of Bosch; the 2nd. display case contains the forementioned triptych on wood by Gerard David; another wood painting of interest is the *Moneychanger* and his Wife, by Marinus Reymerswaele († 1567), signed in 1538 and inspired on another composition by Quintín Metsys in the Louvre, and the *Betrothal of St. Catalina,* school of Malinas.

In the first small room, at the back, is a large *Calvary,* a XVth Century Gothic cloth with the technique "of wavy trimmings and fringes", but painted instead of embroidered. The showcases contain water painting studies of Natural History by Durero, now restored by Asensio. In the left hand showcase there are: *fish, frogs, dragon flies and crabs; birds and insects* (2 different sketches); *lily, owl* (incomplete); in the showcase on the right: *bats, birds, monkeys and birds of prey; landscape of the Valle de Isaxeo.* As well as the *Insults* by el Bosco, in the second little hall is exhibited *Rest in the Flight to Egypt,* attributed to Quintín Metsys (1465-1530) and other *Temptations of St. Anthony,* also from the school of Bosch. The first Hall, with its little rooms, corresponds to the rooms of Philip II's favourite daughter, the Infanta Isabel Clara Eugenia, which are on the upper floor.

Room II. Here are displayed works by the Mannerist Miguel Coxcie, the splendid Flemish painter (1499-1592) who worked so much for El Escorial; the *Triptych of the Story of St. Philip* with *the Martyrdom of the Saint* (centre), *His Preaching* (right) *and His Arrest* (left); *The Annunciation, the Virgin with the Child, St. Joaquín and St. Ann; the Virgin and St. Joseph prostrate, adoring the Child; Oblation to the Child Jesus* and *the Holy Supper.*

Room III contains almost entirely works by Titian (1477-1576), all of them of extraordinary value such as the *Burial of Christ; Christ Crucified Whose Redeeming Blood is Collected by Three Angels; Christ Shown to the People by Pilate* (Ecce Homo), a masterpiece of El Escorial; *The Prayer in the Garden* and *St. Hieronymo in Prayer.* Apart from the Titianesque series, there are also the *Rest in the Flight to Egypt,* and the *Adoration of the Kings,* by Bassano (1549-1592) and *Noli Me Tangere,* a copy from el Veronés by Lucas Jordán (1632-1705) and *Jesus and the Samaritan.*

Habitaciones de la Infanta Isabel Clara Eugenia
Appartements de l'Infante Isabelle Claire Eugénie
Apartments of the Infanta Isabel Clara Eugenia

Gemaecher der Prinzessin Isabel Clara Eugenia
Camere dell'Infanta Isabella Clara Eugenia
Habitaçoes da Infanta Isabel Clara Eugénia

Juan Pantoja de la Cruz: Felipe II anciano
Juan Pantoja de la Cruz: Philippe II âge
Juan Pantoja de la Cruz: Philip II as an old man

Juan Pantoja de la Cruz: Filip II Greis
Juan Pantoja de la Cruz: Filippo II vecchio
Juan Pantoja de la Cruz: Felipe II anciao

Juan Pantoja de la Cruz: Felipe II anciano
Juan Pantoja de la Cruz: Philippe II âgé
Juan Pantoja de la Cruz: Philip II as an old man
Juan Pantoja de la Cruz: Filip II Greis
Juan Pantoja de la Cruz: Filippo II vecchio
Juan Pantoja de la Cruz: Felipe II anciao

179

Habitaciones de Felipe II
Appartements de Philippe II
Apartments of Philip II

Gemaecher Filips II
Camere di Filippo II
Habitações de Felipe II

Tapices flamencos
Tapisseries flamandes
Flemish tapestries

Flamische Wanntppiche
Arazzi fiamminghi
Tapête flamengos

Sala de la Silla de Manos. Siglo XVI
Salle de la chaise à porteurs. XVIe siècle
Room of the Pedanchair. XVIth Century

Saal des Tragesessels. XVI Jahrh
Sala della Sedia a Mano. Sec. XVI
Sala da Liteira. S. XVI

El Greco: Detalle-busto de San Ildefonso
Le Greco: Détail de Saint Ildefonse
The Greco: Detail of St. Ildephonse

Der Greco: Der heilige Ildefons (Detail)
Il Greco: Particolare del busto di Sant´Ildefonso
O Greco: Pormenor-busto de São Ildefonso

The Great *Room IV,* which corresponds to the Throne Room of the main part of the building "is one of the most beautiful museum halls in Europe because of the typical El Escorial atmosphere of walls patterned with glazed tiles and big windows looking out over the Jardín de los Frailes and also because of the exceptional quality of the works displayed" (Lozoya). They are magnificent examples of the Venetian School and of Italian works; the most outstanding collection is formed by the works of Titian: *The Last Supper* and *St. John the Baptist;* there is a splendid series by Tintoretto (Jacopo Robusti, 1518-1594): *The Magdalene annointing the Lord's Feet in the Pharisee's House; Magdalene Penitent; Burial of Christ; Queen Esther fainting before Asuero;* and *the Nativity with the Adoration of the Shepherds;* an *Ecce Homo* is also attibuted to him. There are other capital works by el Veronés (Paolo Caliari, 1528?-1588), such as the *Annunciation,* or the *Appearance of Christ to His Mother Accompanied by the Fathers of Limbo,* and *The Father and the Holy Spirit.* The other paintings are: *Lot and his family leaving Sodom led by an Angel,* by Andres Vaccaro (1598-1670); *The Departure of Abraham* (with his family and cattle for the Land of Canaan by the command of the Lord) and the *Emmaus Supper* by Bassano (Giacomo da Ponte 1510-15-1592); *Christ Bearing the Cross,* by Guido Reni (1575-1642); *Baptism of Christ* and *St. Hieronymo* attributed to Palma the Younger (1544-1628); the *Adoration of the Kings* and the *Adoration of the Shepherds,* by Federico Zúccaro (1542-43-1609); and a *Descent,* also from the Venetian School.

Room V is dedicated to the works of the great Spanish painter José de Ribera (1591-1652), among which are some of his best works; three *St. Hieronymo Penitent* (half-body and profile, full lenght grasping some ropes to lift himself up, and with a skull in his hand); *St. Anthony;* and *Jacob grazing the flocks of Laban* **(p. 151),** (two of his ouststanding works); *St. Francis; Burial of Christ; The Hermit King* (St. Onofre?); *St. Paul; The Philosopher Crisipo; St. John the Baptist as a Child* and *Aesop the fable writer.*

Between *Rooms V and VI* in a cupboard, with glass on two of its sides, are displayed various models of Talavera delft produced for the needs of the Monastery; ink wells, jugs, plates, bowls, deep bowls, earthen pans, glazed tiles for socles, shelves and surfaces forming angles (XVI and XVIIth Century).

Room VI forms the ensemble of a room with direct light looking out over the garden, and two smaller rooms. These correspond on the upper floor to the rooms of Philip II. It also contains works from the XVIIth Century Spanish School; the capital painting is the one by Diego Velázquez (1599-1660); *Joseph's brothers present their father Jacob with a bloody tunic, which they claim is Joseph's* **(p. 152)** painted (like *Vulcan's Forge)* whilst Velázquez was staying in Rome in 1630. Somewhat separated from it, despite their interest, are *The Presentation of the Virgin in the Temple,* by Zurbarán workshop; *the Birth of the Virgin,* by Juan de Valdés Leal (1622-1690); *Virgin with child,* attributed to Alonso Cano (1601-1667); *David as a young man,* Murillesque; and a *View of the Palace of Aceca* by Juan Bautista del Mazo († 1667). In the little room on the left is exhibited a portrait of *Charles II as a child,* from the workshop of Juan Carreño (1614-1685) and a *St. Peter of Alcántara,* anonymous. In the little room on the right is a portrait of *Philip IV,* by Antonio Arias († 1684), and two of his wife *Queen Doña Mariana de Austria* (as a young lady, also by Arias and another when she is older and wearing a widows bonnet, from the workshop of Juan Carreño).

Rooms VII, VIII and IX are around the beautiful Courtyard of the Masks from which they receive futher light, and in them is a collection of secondary works from the Italian and Flemish schools with some examples of methods of study for a just evaluation and possible attributions.

Room VII contains paintings from the Italian School, some of which are very notable, such as the *Prophet Isaiah* and the *Eritrean Sibyl,* masterpieces by Alessandro Boncivino, called Moretto de Brescia (1498-1554); and the one entitled *Mystical Subject, Christ, grown up and beardless,* the Virgin and St. Peter Martyr of Verona, (impetrate God the Father on behalf of three penitents), by Mariotto Albertinelli (1474-1515); completing the collection there are anonymous grisailles, *Christ Descending from Limbo* and *Resurrection; Madonna or Virgin with Child* and another *Virgin with Child and little St. John,* a copy of Raphael by Nicolás Poussin (1594-1665).

Room VIII also displays works from the Italian School: *Descent* (school of Veronés); *Lot drunken by his daughters,* by Guercino (1591-1665); *Virgin with the Child and little Sr. John,* called the Virgin of the Oak-Tree, attributed to Pordenone (?); and an *Ecce Homo* by G. B. Crespi (1576-1632).

Room IX contains a variety of works, as many from the Italian School as from the Flemish and Dutch schools, such as two excellent *Stil Life paintings with pomegranates, pears and grapes;* and *pears, plums and apples pecked by some birds,* both on canvas glued to wood, attributed to the Dutch Jan Davidsz de Heen (1606-1683-84); two *flower pots in a vaulted recess* by Daniel Seghers (1590-1661); a *Holy Family,* from the Italian School; *Virgin with the Child;* another *Virgin with the Child* from the school of Van Dyck; another *Still Life* from the Flemish Georg Van-Son (1623-1667), with lobster, lemon, grapes, peaches...; and the gem of the Room: *Emmaus Supper,* by Pedro Pablo Rubens (1577-1640), sketch painting preserved in the Prado Museum.

By the same staircase which leads to the floor of vaulted ceilings, where the Museum of Architecture is installed, one reaches the galleries which surround the so-called main Court of the Palace; there, in two large vaulted rooms, habe been collected various canvasses of capital importance which, because of their size, could not be fitted into the relatively small rooms in Philip II's Summer Palace, which has just been described. The first of these beautiful rooms is called the *Hall of Honour,* and is dedicated to the glory of the founder King. In it stands out impressively the *Martyrdom of St. Maurice and the Theban Legion* **(p. 149-166),** a masterpiece by Domenico Theotocopuli, el Greco (1541-1614), and one of the most extraordinary paintings in the world; the present situation of this most important of the paintings in El Escorial, allows all its exceptional qualities to be appreciated; "Now can one contemplate it with sufficient perspective and with the right amount of light to savour the accumulation of marvels which make up the brilliant work" (Lozoya). In it are depicted the various episodes in the martyrdom decreed by the Emperor Maximiano Hercules who ordered the massacre of all those who belonged to the Theban legion, starting with their leader St. Maurice, and down to the last of his soldiers, all of them Christians, because they refused to take part in the sacrifices to the gods which were ordered by the Emperor, whom the Legion accompanied to the Galias to fight the rising legions. Maximian Hercules ordered the Legion twice to be decimated, but as they would not give up their faith, he ordered their entire massacre in the year of Our Lord 286. The vivid colour and most original composition, placing the martyrs in various groups, and the angels on high in a glimpse of Glory, make the magnificent canvas even more pathetic.

In the same room can be admired another beautiful painting, the great *Calvary* by Roger Vander Weyden (1399-1464),

(p. 162), as well as the magnificent copy of the masterpiece of the same famous Flemish painter, *The Descent,* painted by Miguel Coxcie by order of Philip II, who paid him in 1569. The original, painted about 1435 for the Chapel of the Archers of Louvain, was acquired by Mary of Hungary, sister of Charles V, and sent to Spain. Philip II placed it in El Escorial in 1574; today it is preserved in the Prado Museum.

The wall at the back of this Hall, opposite the windows, is adorned with a great tapestry belonging to the *Conquest of Tunis* series, one of the most famous of Brussels tapestries and without doubt the most famous work of the tapestry maker, Guillermo Pannemaker, who finished it in 1554. Ten cloths are preserved, although there were twelve in the series, and the most beautiful of all is the one which depicts (the second in the series) and expounds the *Review of the Expeditionary Force in Barcelona by Charles V,* accompanied by Court personages and by the Emperor's guard (14th May, 1535). As originality in this tapestry, the novelty of the composition should be pointed out. It seeks to effect wide perspectives like a true picture of battles; also the exclusive right to put large letters of explanation in Spanish, which appear on the top of the edges (Sánchez Cantón) is very original. In the lower part, there are also large Latin verses which similarly comment on the subject. On the opposite wall, another precious tapestry from the XVIth Century, although much smaller in size, depicts the *Jardín de las Delicias,* for which the triptych of the same subject by el Bosco served as a model. To complete the decoration of this Hall is a showcase containing the *sword and ruff of Charles V* and various *documents* which refer to El Escorial and to the King: the *autographed letter from Philip II* telling his father the Emperor of the success of the Battle of San Quintín (28th August, 1557); (Archive of Simancas); *the document of*

endowment of the Foundation of the Monastery of El Escorial,
signed on 28th April, 1567; *the testament sealed by Philip II,*
in Madrid, on the 7th March, 1594; and the Codicil granted by
the Monarch, with the date 23th August, 1597, the three documents are kept in the Archive of the Palace in Madrid. And
above an Italian table, encrusted with carved ivory, representing mythological scenes, there is displayed a valuable engraved iron chest, these last with figures from pagan mythology or
allegories according to the taste of the time (XVIth Century).
Two suits of armour with pikes, also from the XVIth Century,
one of the Infante and the other of a rider, each one on a
dummy, appearing to mount guard in the great Hall **(p. 149).**

The Pinacotheca ends with the so-called *Hall of el Greco or
of the Grecos* because in it are displayed the rest of the paintings by the brilliant artist from Toledo, in a dazzling polychromy which stands out most beautifully in the grandiose simplicity of this vaulted room, returned to its original beauty and se-
verity, characteristic of Herrera, by one of the most pleasant
restorations completed in the new ensemble of El Escorial museums by the architect of the Patrimonio, D. Ramón Andrada.
These paintings are the *Adoration of the Name of Jesus* **(p. 167),**
in which appears King Philip II, kneeling among a crowd of
other people, with Glory and Hell. The painting is commonly
called *The Dream of Philip II,* for no reason at all, as it alludes
to the passage from the Epistle of St. Paul to the Philippians:
"in the Name of Jesus, every knee is bowed in the Heavens, on
earth and in Hell." The splendid polychromy and the bold composition are now admired in all their magnificence. *St. Eugenio* (also called *St. Ildefonso,* since both names appear in the
old inventaries), one of the most beautiful and delicate of the
paintings by El Greco **(p. 184)** as well as *St. Peter,* another
masterpiece **(p. 168)** and the two paintings of *St. Francis.*

Accompanying these there are two pictures with the same theme, *the Adoration of the Kings,* attributed to the two Veronés, father and son, Paolo and Carlo († 1596). A valuable Flemish tapestry from the series of the Spheres (XVIth Century), the one here being the *Terrestrial Sphere* accompanied by Jupiter and June, completes the contents of this most beautiful room.

A simple enumeration of the collection of Paintings in the new Halls, as has been made here, seems cold, on account of its necessary brevity, when confronted with the grandiose mastery, the fabulous value in the exceptional qualities of most of the canvasses which have been mentioned. But even this brief enumeration gives some idea of the extraordinary artistic importance of the collection of paintings preserved in the Monastery of El Escorial; the masterpieces are superb next to the productions of secondary value which, even qualified in this way, can be considered as excellent.

The Museum of architecture of the Monastery

The area in which the Museum has been installed was called by its architect, Juan de Herrera, "floor of vaulted ceilings" and is formed by the passage which extends from the rooms on the northern side of the Summer Palace of Philip II to the Tower of Las Damas (N.E.). Destined for centuries as a lumber and storage room, it was completely disfigured by enclosures and separations, but the restoration and cleaning of these additions has resulted in an ensemble of a strong and beautiful construction, "a most adequate showcase for the exhibition of the studies and works of a glorious epoch in our architecture, perhaps the most representative of the Spanish genre" (González Valcárcel). This Museum consists of six spacious vaulted rooms, a gallery equally vaulted, divided into three rectangular spans and two squares; the ensemble is linked to the Palace area by two staircases and a visit to it during the itinerary of the Monastery is both easy and convenient. Its installation, respecting the original architecture of the rooms has been very simple, but very modern, uniting, evaluating and projecting in an orderly fashion the elements and details needed to study in all its aspects the gigantic work of the construction of the Monastery **(p. 161).**

Room 1 : Equipment of the Craftsmen. The craftsmen were not only those who worked materially on the works, but those who represented many professions: politics, with King Philip II at the head, theologists and humanists, architects and assistants, masters in all specialities; painters and sculptors, botanists, doctors, musicians..., in such a way that there was scarcely no profession or social class which was not represented in the work of El Escorial during the 21 years it lasted. With an orderly and patient work they forged great new aesthetic solutions for the old techniques already forgotten. They anticipated solutions for the aesthetic and technical problems of today, and also for the social questions and rational organization of the work, which characterized our age. Following is a record of these craftsmen: Juan de Herrera, architect and mathematician; Benito Arias Montano, theologist and humanist; Fr. Antonio de Villacastín, master of the works; P. José Sigüenza, first historian of the Monastery; the painters Peregrín Tibaldi, Lázaro Tavarone, Lucas Cambiasso, Luchetto, Navarrete el Mudo; Federico Zúccaro, el Bosco, el Greco, Miguel Coxcie, Titian, Tintoretto; the sculptors León Leoni and Juan de Arfe; the lapidary Jácome de Trezzo. When effigies of these

Casita del Príncipe y Jardín
La maison du Prince, vue des jardins
Prince´s Cottage and garden

Blick auf das Untere Prinzenpalais
Palazzino del Principe e giardino
Casinha do Príncipe e Jardim

Vista parcial del zaguán
Aperçu sur un angle du vestibule
Partial view of the entrance hall

Teilansicht des Vestibüls (unten)
Veduta parziale dell'entrata
Vista parcial do Vestíbulo

Sala de la Torre   Der Hauptsaal
Salle de la Tour   Sala della Torre
Tower Room   Sala da Torre

Comedor
La salle à manger
Dining-room

Der Speisesaal
Sala da Pranzo
Sala de Jantar

Sala denominada de Corrado Giacquinto
Salle dite de Corrado Giacquinto
The Giaquinto room

Salon mit Gemälden Corrado Giaquintos.
Sala considdetta di Corrado Giaquinto
Sala denominada de Corrado Giacquinto

197

Fachada principal y jardín
Façade principale et jardin
Main façade and garden

Die Eingangsseite und der Vorgarten
Facciata principale e giardino
Fachada principal e Jardim

Despacho
Le Bureau
Office

Das Arbeitszimmer
Studio
Escritório

Angulo de la Saleta
Angle du petit-salon
Corner of "la Saleta"

Der Salon, Teilansicht
Angolo della Saletta
Ângulo da Saleta

craftsmen are not displayed, their names are gathered on beautiful Xilographic engraved tablets with allegories of Architecture, Painting and Sculpture, figuring on them according to their respective profession; such are the names of Juan Bautista de Toledo, the first architect; Monegro and Pompeyo Leoni, sculptors; Francisco de Mora, architect; the painters Luis de Carvajal, Juan and Martín Gómez, Juan Bautista Castello, el Bergamasco, Rómulo Cincinatto, Rodrigo de Holanda, and Fabricio Castello, Nicolás Granello, Horacio Cambiasso, Miguel Barroso, Francisco de Urbina, Bartolomé Carduccio, Juan Pantoja de la Cruz.

Room II: The Building. In this room are exhibited numerous details of economic character concerning *the costs* of the different parts of the work and the sum total, spent in the whole construction, in the money of the time, and its present day equivalent in pesetas; diverse engravings and drawings stand out in a greenish tone to illustrate each one of the parts corresponding to its respective cost. There are also on display some *plans* of the general organization of the architectonic work and of the organization of the Treasury or economy. In a showcase are displayed various documents referring to the work; general instruction given by the King Philip II, in 1572 —drafts, payrolls; perforated slips of paper to deposit in archives, in which appeared the sums paid to the workmen and purveyors; and the *Diary of the works,* a manuscript autographed by Fr. Juan de San Jerónimo, as well as an exemplar of the *History of the Order of St. Hieronymo,* by Fr. José de Sigüenza (second edition—Madrid, 1600), which deals with the foundation and construction of the Monastery.

Room III: Plans by Juan de Herrera and his disciples for the construction of El Escorial. A great number of plans, designs and sketches attributed to the architect Juan de Herrera, a man of exceptional artistic and mathematical quality, have been displayed. The collection is preserved in the Royal Palace in Madrid and was published by the Patrimonio Nacional in 1945. The sketches exhibited are: Section of the church by its main axis; plan of the church, its foundations, its columns and its tower by the side of the Epistle; study for the cornice of the church; plan of one of the towers; plan of the angular tower corresponding to the Prioral cell; rough sketch of the altar of Relics; sketch of the small courtyards in the Monastery, plans for the works of passages which divide up the courtyard in the Royal Palace; of the paving of the main staircase; plan for the Pantheon of Kings; six plans of the royal apartments on the eastern side; enclosure of the Lonja; Section of the Monastery mill; sketch for the second house of offices, its lower floor, its definite plan, and that of the second floor.

Room IV: Engravings by Pierre Perret. This Flemish engraver and designer (Amberes 1555 - Madrid 1624-25) came to Madrid in 1583 from Rome, where he worked to improve and perfect his art, and was commissioned by Juan de Herrera to engrave in copper the designs he had made for the Monastery of San Lorenzo de El Escorial with a view to letting the world know of so grandiose a work, in a collection of copper plates so much in vogue at the time. Perret worked on them from 1583 to 1589. This year he entered the service of the King and in 1595, Philip II named him engraver of the royal works. These *copper plates* are: 1) first and general plan of the entire building; 2) second general plan; 3) Orthography (raised) of the entrance to the temple and interior section of the convent and college; 4) Orthography and interior section of the temple with its retable and high altar and convent cloisters and Royal House; 5) Orthography and interior section of the temple and part of the temple and royal rooms; 6) exterior southern orthography of the temple and royal rooms (southern facade); 7) general perspective; 8) high retable; 9) Pyx by Jácome Trezzo; 10) Section of the interior of same; 11) 1. Monstrance, 2. Plan of the pyx; 12) Perspective of the Chapel and High Altar.

The copper engravings belong to the Library collection of the Royal Palace in Madrid, except for the Perspective of the retable in the Main Chapel, which belongs to the section of Fine Arts in the National Library. A valuable original drawing by Herrera of the southern facade of the Monastery which also belongs to the Section already mentioned should also be added.

Room V: Iconography of the Monastery. Engravings. The Monastery is, without doubt, one of the most famous buildings in the world. Even before its completion, drawings and engravings were already being circulated round all the Courts in Europe, which began to divulge its well-known shilhouette of an inverted gridiron. Each period of the romantic Baroque art has had El Escorial as one of its favourite themes.

In this room are displayed some examples of how El Escorial has been seen in different epochs; in a showcase may be found its reproduction in different books; in the *Theatrum Orbis Terrarum,* by Abraham Ortelio (Anvers Officina Plantiniana, 1602); in the *Brief Description of the Monastery of San Lorenzo el Real de El Escorial, Unique Wonder of the World,* by Padre Francisco de los Santos (Madrid, 1657), published when the Kings' Pantheon was inaugurated; in the *Geografia Blaviana, Spain* (Amsterdam, Juan Blaeu, 1672), with the arrival of the Court at El Escorial; in the second volume of the *Annales de l'Espagne et de Portugal,* by Juan Alvarez de Colmenar (Amsterdam, 1741); and in the 4th edition (Madrid, 1698) of the *Brief Description of the Monastery of San Lorenzo el Real,* by Padre Francisco de los Santos.

In similar copper engravings are the romantic collections of
different views of the exterior and interior of the Monastery;
ones engraved with a burin by López Enguídanos, following the
sketches of José Gómez de Navia and another formed by the
lithographies made by Asselineau over paintings by Francisco
Brambilla. Both collections belong to the Library of the Royal
Palace in Madrid. On one of the walls of the Room, two frescoe
paintings represent Philip II carrying a rose in his hand, a symbol of Architecture and before him are grouped some of the ar-
tisans of El Escorial: Herrera, Fr. Antonio de Villacastín, Trezzo
and Benito Arias Montano, the work signed by the architect and
painter Joaquín "Vaquero Turcios, 1963".

Room VI: Iconography. Contains some paintings of the time
and later ages, such as the perspective of the Monastery on
the wood painting of the Dutch Isaac Jacob Swanenburgh,
from the XVIth Century (Collection González Valcárcel); the
anonymous copper work from the XVIIth Century which served
as the poster for the centenary celebrations in 1963; the painting alluding to the triumphs of Philip V over his rival the Arch-
duke of Austria, or *Philip V, conqueror of Heresy,* accompanied
by Faith and Queen Maria Luisa of Savoy, first wife of the
monarch, with her son Prince D. Luis. Between the married
couple is the Monastery of El Escorial; in the sky, the Virgin of
the Patronage between St. Hieronymous and St. Lorenzo; the
painting is attributed to Felipe de Silva (XVIIIth Century); from
the XIXth Century are the paintings by Fernando Branbilla:
*Interior of the temple with the Monument of Holy Week; the
Monastery from the east side; the Court of the Evangelists;* and
the View of the Monastery from the east and south, by Francisco Van Halen (1851). One can also admire the wooden project
given by the Museum of Architecture by the Superior School of
Architecture in Madrid. Also exhibited is a copper engraving de-

picting the *Holy Family,* which appeared in one of the lantern shades when its present repair was begun; it seems to be by Juan Francisco Romanelli (1617-1663).

Room VII: Tools. In this room are displayed various collections of tools which were used in the construction of the Monastery, all of them coming from various palaces of the Patrimonio Nacional. Many of them, which are not used today, have evolved with similar forms. The most important ones are the following: a *large sword* of the stonemason, with smooth leaves and leaves in the shape of a saw. They were used to spread the mortar made of lime between the building blocks and to scrape and clean the unions between the *Mixers* where the lime was prepared. Small hand trowels. *Saws,* for wood, handled by two men. *Ladles* of various sizes, to smelt the lead and other kinds of metals. *Chisels,* for engraving stone. *Drills,* for boring in the soil. *Tracers* for stone masonry and carpentry. *Pitchforks, prickers, pick-axes* and *rakes, for lime ovens. Needles* or *little nails,* used for alignment. *Rammers, hinges* with various mouth shapes. *Little seals. Fringes.*

Room VIII. Materials. Here one may appreciate the first constructive materials which were used to raise El Escorial.

Granite from the neighbourhood of the Monastery. Two kinds of grains were used, the fine ones for the ornaments. The quarries of Bernardos (Avila) were opened to supply this original material. *Ceramic. Brick* from local clay; the so-called "Cántaro", finer, for the friezes and the visible arches. *Glazed tiles,* used as socles for the main royal apartments. *Slate* used to cover the roofs. This material was first used in Spain for El Escorial. Workmen from Flanders had to come and teach how it was joined.

Room IX. Carpentry Shop. The perfection to which all the different kinds of constructive works in El Escorial aspired, is displayed in this exhibition of carpentry which is on show. Carpentry from the work-shop, but so well made that it seems more like the work of a cabinet maker. It contains the following:

Project for the frame of the capital of the Tower of Las Damas, constructed to scale with old woods, for this Museum. *Plans for the Tower frame,* with constructive details of the original, authentic, *joints* of the structures of the towers, which have had to be replaced by works because of the invasion —"termites"— which the Monastery recently suffered. *Clasps* for the joints of "Jupiter's Lightning", of forged iron, made for the nave of the capital. *Nails* of different kinds used in the construction, from those of great size to those "like the wing of a fly", to affix the slate tiles. *Doors,* low shutters with balconies weighing a quarter of a pound, in Spanish style. There are two, one complete ànd the other in pieces, in which one may appreciate the true delicacy of this carpentry.

Room X. Professions. Among the professions which contributed to this great work, some are displayed here.

The locksmith, with a curious collection of old keys. The *leadworker* with various kinds of ways in which lead is used in the covers. *Glass,* with samples of the various kinds of glass which were used, and the fabrication of silica brought from La Granja. *Iron,* with balustrades for staircases railings and balconies. *Silver* brought from the mines of Linares; it was used in great quantity for silverwork in the sacred cult. *Gold* abundantly used in the retables, railings and architectonic details.

Room XI: Machines. Juan de Herrera was not only a great architect, but also an inventor of "machines" which were quite ahead of his time. His famous "pen" is a true crane which he invented by himself. In this room one may admire (1):

Memorial by Herrera to Philip II "of the Machine", in which he explains the function and necessity for the *"pen"* or *crane*

(Monastery Library). Pen: the dummy for this crane was made recently according to Herrera's designs, with wood from the time of the construction of the Monastery. *Tongs* of great size to lift the stone blocks, one of them supporting the block of granite; *pulleys* of different forms and sizes, with ropes and hooks of the time. *Tripods. Photograph,* large size, of the drawing of 1576, in which the Monastery appears half built. In it one can clearly see how the "pens", invented by Herrera, worked. Legend of the engraving: "The King of Spain's House" (Col. Lord Burghley, London, now in the British Museum).

Because of the variety of its content, the grandiosity of each of its ensembles, the richness of its artistic collections, the innumerable historical suggestions, the beauty of its topographical situation, a visit to San Lorenzo de El Escorial will be one of the memories which will last in the minds of its visitors.

---

(1) The description of Rooms VII to XI, corresponds almost word for word with the Catalogue which the architects Carlos de Miguel Javier Fecuchi and Jesus Bosch, under the supervision of the Director General of Architecture D. Miguel Angel García Lomas, published for the inauguration of the Museum.

THE PRINCE'S LITTLE HOUSE

It is a small building close to the railway station, in the bottom of the valley formed by the slopes of the Sierra de Guadarrama mountains, among luxuriant groves. It is so called because it was built for the crown prince, Don Carlos, Prince of Asturias at the time, and later Charles IV. During his time it was also known as the *Prince's Casino*, since it was a place for amusement, and also as *Casita de Abajo,* to differentiate it from another one also located in the neighbourhood of the Monastery, but in the West, owned by the Infante Don Gabriel, the Prince's brother, and known as the *Casita de Arriba.*

In the year 1772, Don Carlos commissioned the architect Don Juan de Villanueva to build him a *little house* or *Casino* in a piece of land he owned on the eastern side of the Monastery of San Lorenzo. It was also the Prince's fondest wish to have this *little house* decorated and ornamented with all kinds of beautiful and artistic objects; in order to do so he collected paintings of notable merit, exquisite furniture and clocks, valuable ornamental pieces, tapestry and rugs from the Royal Factory of Santa Bárbara in Madrid; lovely chandeliers and lamps and two outstanding sets of porcelains, both from the workshops of the Royal Factory of the Buen Retiro; an abundant collec-

tion of 226 porcelains in the British Wedgwood style (white reliefs on a blue background) in the shape of small plaques,
framed like small pictures, with mythological scenes, baskets
and bouquest, vases, silhouetted busts and other ornaments;
and another precious series of ivory reliefs, exquisitely carved, as well as beautiful figures of the same fine material,
true masterpieces of miniature work on account of the exquisite taste and superior ability of the artists who executed them.

For his part, the architect built a simple structure of grey
granite, the floor plan in the shape of a T, consisting of a
centre tower connected on three of its sides, North, South and
West to three rectangular wings; in the front elevation are two
floors, the upper one smaller in height, three windows on each
floor and sides of the main facade; the centre or nucleus is
thus, the highest part forming a small tower with slate roofing
ending in the middle. The façade faces east **(p. 193),** is 27
metres wide and is divided into three parts; its only ornaments
are simple brackets and dust guards on the ground floor and a
narrow cornice that marks the upper floor by means of a small
projection. The most beautiful part of the facade is the elegant
and salient portico in the centre of which is the entrance to the
little house; on a base of three steps rise four Tuscan columns
supporting a very simple entablature which, surrounded by an
iron railing, forms a spacious balcony projecting over the cornice; the western facade, much narrower since it corresponds
to the small side of the rectangle, has a small porch in the
centre supported also by two Tuscan columns.

To such simple, although elegant exterior, corresponds a
beautiful interior composed by a series of rooms in their most
part reduced in size, richly covered with embroidered or brocade silks from the time of Charles IV and his son Ferdinand VII,
some having been restored following the neo-classical and

Empire style. A notable group is that of the paintings on the ceiling, almost all, in Pompeian style so diversified that each room varies elegantly from the rest; the painters were: Juan Duque, Jacinto Gómez Pastor, Manuel Pérez and Felipe López; the ceilings were decorated with gilded stucco by Ferroni (the dining room) and the brothers Pablo and Mateo Brilli. The floors are generally in black and white marble slabs as well as polychrome marble, and the staircase and some of the rooms in the upper floor in jasper; but the most beautiful floors are those of the so-called "of fine woods", on account of their being made of exquisite inlays and marketry of different colours, precious woods forming foliage and flowers, urns and other ornamente (three consecutive rooms in the first landing of the staircase). Marble and jasper were also used in many of the socles in the different rooms.

Because of its richness and beauty the *Prince's Little House* soon became famous and was greatly admired; unfortunately the Napoleonic invasion severely damaged the Royal Residences, and many of the valuable objects kept in them disappeared; this also happened in the *Little House* from whence many of the precious possessions which were kept in it disappeared. Ferdinand VII tried to make of this small palace the place of amusement and rest that his father, Charles IV, had meant it to be and restored, refurnished and re-decorated some of its rooms with the ostentatious taste of his time (Empire style) collecting once more in the *Little House* as many works of art as could be found, that had belonged to it. In the appraisal made by order of the Monarch at that time, the building with its wooded lands and the precious objects in it was assessed at 150 million reales ($37^1/_2$ million pesetas).

During the Regency of Doña María Cristina de Borbón, the widow of Ferdinand VII, fearing the factions from the province

of Toledo and the Valley of Tiétar, the major section of the
pictures in the *Prince's Little House* were taken to Madrid for
safety purposes and placed in the Royal Museum of Paintings
(Prado). During the successive reigns nothing in particular
affected the Little House until the time of Alphonso XII
with the timely restoration of the ceilings. After the Spanish
War of Liberation the aggregate of buildings of El Escorial came
under the protection of H.E. the Chief of State, Generalísimo
Don Francisco Franco who later created the Patrimonio Nacional, a high governing body that was to direct and administer the
old crown properties, and which was in charge of carefully
attempting to correct the effect of time.

Thus, today, once more the *Prince's Little House* is a gra-
cious and beautiful palace surrounded by gardens and wooded
lands, a pleasant and tranquil place, exhibiting once more beautiful paintings, furniture, chandeliers, clocks, porcelains, ivories,
sculptures and decorative silks. As in all the antique Sites and
Royal Palaces, the value of these collections is also that of its
authenticity: most of the things that may be admired in the
Little House were expressly made for the place where they are
now kept. Only some of the paintings are not the same ones
which were in its rooms originally since they have come to form
part of the collection of the first National Museum, the Prado
Museum, or of the apartments of the Royal Palace in Madrid,
places which were considered more adequate for their keeping
and for public viewing.

The tourist's visit to the *Prince's Little House* at present
covers the group of rooms on the main floors, a total of 11: the
Vestibule **(p. 194)** from whence the visit of the rooms to the
left of the entrance is initiated; in the *first room* (2nd. counting
the *Vestibule)* is exhibited an interesting collection of paintings
by Lucas Jordán, some dealing with Mythological subjects *(The*

Rape of Proserpine by Pluto, Proserpine and Pluto, the Fall of Phaeton); and some religious ones *(Christ appearing before Mary Magdalene);* or historical *(The Rape of the Sabines, Semiramis)* **(p. 195);** in the *second room* among the various flower pieces and still life paintings which ornament it, may be admired *Bodegón de la Sandía,* by López Enguídanos in which stands out the transparency of a glass full of water. Next, in the *third room* can be admired the beautiful collection of paintings also by Lucas Jordán, Allegories of the Virtues *(Charity, Fortitude, Temperance)* and *Parts of the World* (Europe, Asia, Africa and America). It should be noticed that the *Prince's Little House* constitutes one of the numerous and important depositories of the paintings of the Italian master of this XVIIth Century and of another great painter of the XVIIIth Century, also Italian, Corrado Giaquinto **(p. 197).**

The *fourth Room* is a small chamber through which one may pass to the *corridor;* two paintings of great interest should be noticed: *St. Catherine* by Guido Reni and *St. Cecilien* by Dominico Zampieri, "el Dominiquino".

The *Dining Room* **(p. 196)** is the biggest room in the Little House and one of the most luxurious; the walls, drapings and chairs are in green satin; the ceiling is decorated with beautiful white and gold stucco, by Ferroni, the paintings exhibited here are almost all by Lucas Jordán, standing out the three occupying the two main fore parts representing: *The Death of the Apostate Julianus* and the *Conversion of St. Paul,* admirable in movement, colouring and strength; also by him is an *Immaculate Conception.*

The furnishings are Empire style and among them must be mentioned the great mahogany table in the centre, with Spanish marble mosaic supported by 16 Corinthian columns with gilded bronze capitals; the underside of the top presents skilled

workmanship carved and gilded, which may be admired due
to the fact that the table has a lower platform with mirrors
which reflect it. This piece of furniture is not truly a dining-room
piece, but rather served to exhibit a cut-glass table service
given to Ferdinand VII; a great 48 light chandelier in cut-glass
and gilded bronze completes the decoration.

The dining room opens to the oval *Coffee Room;* it occupies
the rear of the Dining Room which corresponds to the West
side; it is oval in shape as its name indicates, and between the
doors and the windows open four recesses with four white marble sculptures imitating antique busts of the Roman Emperors;
the walls and ceiling of this room are of beautiful white stucco
with gilded ornaments and reliefs, the work of Pablo and Mateo
Brilli; in the centre of it, and on top of a bureau is an alabaster
shrine with a circular base and a cupola, beautifully carved,
with a bust of Ferdinand VII inside.

In order to visit the rooms on the right hand side, the Vestibule must be reached again. These rooms stand out with an excellent collection of paintings which continues in the last of the
rooms of the lower floor. This room also exhibits curious and
delicate little pictures modelled with rice paste, by Genes. The
paintings by Corrado Giaquinto **(p. 197)** include religious subjects, mythological subjects and allegories; thus the Spanish
Saints *St. Ildefonso, St. Hermegildo, St. Isidro,* farmer and his
wife, *St. Mary of the Head; the Prayer in the Garden; the
Scourging of the Lord; the Crowning of thorns* and *Calvary; the
Goddess Ceres, Adonis, Apollo and Daphne; Allegories of
Abundance* and of *Commerce;* and *Astronomy, Victory,* copies
of the paintings on the staircase of the Royal Palace in Madrid,
are works of the same artist as well as the sketches of some
Mythological Subjects for the same place.

All the rooms contain lovely furniture, rich chandeliers of bronce and cut-glass, candelabrum and beautiful clocks generally Empire style in harmony with the decorations, along with porcelain vases from the Buen Retiro and Sèvres.

HIGHER LITTLE HOUSE

Just like his brother the Prince of Asturias had built the Prince's Little House of *"Casita de Abajo"*, the Infante Don Gabriel de Borbón commissioned the architect, Don Juan de Villánueva, about the same time, to construct another *Little House* or *Casino* **(p. 198)**. Built on the eastern side of the Monastery, and located on a hill, it was thus called the *Casita de Arriba;* its location as if on a balcony, affords it beautiful views. It is smaller and simpler than the *Prince's Little House* and it was never as important nor did it hold the richness and exquisite works of art of the latter.

It consists of a single square structure, all of granite stone, in which two floors are slightly noticed, the upper of little height. The facáde, soberly harmonious, presents a cour or porch with Ionian columns and a complicated crown. The rooms are distributed around a main parlour **(p. 199-200),** a kind of domed rotunda; perhaps the concerts that the Infante was so fond of were held here. It was used as a Summer residence until the time of Ferdinand VII.

It is surrounded by a box garden, and on a lower plane, next to it, a pond or poll was built.

Patrimonio Nacional has recently restored this *Little House,* upholstering it beautifully and placing there some adequate pictures and furniture, also come clocks and cut-glass and bronze chandeliers, some of which were originally in the *"Casita"* resulting in another small pleasant palace, easy to visit. From its beautiful gardens, splendid panoramas may be enjoyed.

PHILIP II'S SEAT

Approximately two kilometres in a straight line from the Monastery, on the hill of the Dehesa del Castañar, at the foot of the mountains known as the Hermits, rises a path on the hillside ending on a crest where large boulders, so abundant in that place, are scattered; some stone seats cut out of the highest point of one of the biggest boulders are known as *Philip II's seat,* because, according to tradition, the Monarch used to go there to watch the construction of the Monastery; this legend does not seem very probable, although he might have enjoyed this place from which beautiful views may be contemplated and an excellent temperature can be enjoyed in the Summer time. Patrimonio Nacional has carried out works to embellish the place and to make it more accessible and comfortable for the visitors **(p. 24).**

INDEX OF ILLUSTRATIONS

GENERAL ALPHABETICAL INDEX

Pages

SEGOVIA

RIOFRIO

LA GRANJA

86 Km.

a Avila

San Rafael

Puerto de Navacerrada

MONUMENTO
NACIONAL A
LOS CAIDOS

Guadarrama

64 Km.

Villalba

ESCORIAL

45 Km.

EL PARDO

Las Rozas

MADRID

a Toledo

70 Km.

47 Km.

ARANJUEZ

TOURISTICAL GUIDES

PATRIMONIO NACIONAL

Madrid. *Royal Orient Palace.*
Madrid. *Royal Armoury.*
Madrid. *Museum of Carriages.*
Madrid. *Monasteries-Museums of the Royal Descalzas and the Church of the Incarnation.*
Madrid. *Moncloa Palace.*
El Pardo (Palace-Museum, House of the Prince and Palace of La Quinta).
Palace-Monastery with the Houses of the Prince and of Arriba at San Lorenzo of El Escorial.
National Monument of Santa Cruz of the Valle de los Caídos.
Aranjuez: *History, Palaces-Museums and Gardens.*
Royal Palace of La Granja and Palace-Residence with the Hunting Museum, in Riofrío. Segovia.
Museum-Monastery of the Huelgas and the Palace of the Isla, in Burgos, *and the Museum-Monastery of Santa Clara at Tordesillas.* Valladolid.
Seville's Royal Alcázares.
Barcelona. *Palace of Pedralbes and Albéniz Small Palace.*

LIBRERIA DEL PATRIMONIO NACIONAL
Plaza de Oriente, 6 (esquina a Felipe V) — Madrid-13

PATRIMONIO NACIONAL

SELECT EDITIONS

EL ESCORIAL
IV CENTENNIAL
(Two volumes)

EL ESCORIAL
EIGHTH WONDER OF THE WORLD

PALACES AND MUSEUMS
OF THE PATRIMONIO NACIONAL

THE ROYAL PALACE OF MADRID

OTHER PUBLICATIONS

MUSEUMS OF MADRID

MUSEUMS OF BARCELONA

MUSEUMS OF SEVILLA

ROYAL COLLECTIONS OF SPAIN
EL MUEBLE

GENERAL ARCHIVE
OF THE ROYAL PALACE OF MADRID

MAGAZINE OF ROYAL PLACES
QUARTERLY PUBLICATION

LIBRERIA EDITORIAL PATRIMONIO NACIONAL   PL. ORIENTE, 6 - MADRID-13

PATRIMONIO NACIONAL

CODICES AND MANUSCRIPTS

HOUR BOOK
OF ISABEL LA CATOLICA

BOOK OF HUNTING
OF THE KING OF CASTILLA ALFONSO XI

ROYAL FESTIVITIES
IN THE REIGN OF FERNANDO VI

THE COUPLES
HORSY PLAY OF THE 18th CENTURY

THE GOLDEN CODEX
THE FOUR EVANGELS

MILITARY THEATRE OF EUROPE
SPANISH UNIFORMS

POEMS OF SANTA MARIA OF ALFONSO X THE WISE, KING OF CASTILLA

CABINET OF LETTERS

TRUJILLO OF THE PERU
AT THE 18th CENTURY (1st volume)

CRONICA TROYANA

BOOK OF CHESS, DICE AND BOARDS OF ALFONSO X THE WISE

FESTIVITIES IN MANILA. YEAR 1825

LIBRERIA EDITORIAL PATRIMONIO NACIONAL   PL. ORIENTE, 6 - MADRID-13